An Integrative Paradigm

SIN AND GRACE
in Christian Counseling

Mark R. McMinn

IVP Academic

An imprint of InterVarsity Press
Downers Grove, Illinois

InterVarsity Press
P.O. Box 1400, Downers Grove, IL 60515-1426
ivpress.com
email@ivpress.com

InterVarsity Press® is the book-publishing division of InterVarsity Christian Fellowship/USA®, a movement of students and faculty active on campus at hundreds of universities, colleges and schools of nursing in the United States of America, and a member movement of the International Fellowship of Evangelical Students. For information about local and regional activities, visit the IVCF website at intervarsity.org.

Unless otherwise indicated, all Scripture quotations are taken from the Holy Bible, New Living Translation, *copyright ©1996, 2004 by Tyndale Charitable Trust. Used by permission of Tyndale House Publishers.*

Design: Cindy Kiple
Images: ©deliormanli/iStockphoto

ISBN 978-0-8308-2851-7

Printed in the United States of America ∞

Library of Congress Cataloging-in-Publication Data

McMinn, Mark R.
 Sin and grace in Christian counseling / Mark R. McMinn.
  p. cm.
 Includes bibliographical references and indexes.
 ISBN-13: 978-0-8308-2851-7 (pbk.: alk. paper)
 1. Pastoral counseling. 2. Sin—Christianity. 3. Grace (Theology)
I. Title.
BV4012.2.M266 2007
253.5—dc22

2007031479

| **P** | 23 | 22 | 21 | 20 | 19 | 18 | 17 | 16 | 15 | 14 | 13 |
| **Y** | 30 | 29 | 28 | 27 | 26 | 25 | 24 | 23 | 22 | 21 | |

Knowing just one person of profound grace might be enough to sustain a person through a meaningful life. I have been deeply blessed to know more than one. This book is dedicated to those dear souls who know me well and still choose to walk alongside as family and friends.

Contents

Acknowledgments. 9

Introduction 11

1 Divided by Sin 15

2 The Weight of Sin. 33

3 The Healing Power of Grace 49

4 Holding Sin and Grace Together—Three Perspectives 73

5 Sin and Grace in Integrative Psychotherapy 92

6 Sin and Grace in the Functional Domain 103

7 Sin and Grace in the Structural Domain 126

8 Sin and Grace in the Relational Domain 148

References 164

Name Index 169

Subject Index 171

Scripture Index 175

Acknowledgments

Some fascinating instinctual force drives salmon to swim upstream and birds to build nests and humans to seek relationships characterized by unmerited kindness. These things draw me to a deep longing to know God, who has always loved creation with a fierce and relentless love. Whatever wisdom can be found in this book is not mine to claim but merely a faint reflection of the great lover of human people.

Somewhere in my thirteen-year sojourn at Wheaton College, I came to love theology. It seems unimaginable now that I once tried to practice psychology as a Christian without knowing much about theology. I am grateful to the many biblical, systematic and historical theologians who have influenced my understanding of the human soul. And the same could be said of those pioneers in the contemporary integration movement—those who have studied both psychology and theology and done justice to both with their writing, clinical work and teaching.

There are people whose names should be listed here, of course. They are colleagues, authors, teachers and students who have inspired and shaped me with their lives and ideas. But as I stare down my fiftieth year of life, there are simply too many positive influences to name. If I were to try, I would leave out several dozen.

My friends have demonstrated grace to me—as friends do—providing the safety to help me explore my weaknesses and strive to become more fully human. Thank you, dear friends. You know who you are even without me listing your names here.

But one name must be mentioned. Lisa, my spouse of twenty-nine years now, is also an author and college professor. I have watched her grow in grace over the years, and I hope she has observed the same in me. What a gift it is to be her life partner. I see many of her fine qualities in our grown daughters, and I marvel how grace finds its way into genetics and home environments and all sorts of other places too.

The team at IVP Academic has been great to work with again as well.

Introduction

A FORMER FACULTY COLLEAGUE ONCE TOLD ME, "Every day I come to work is a day closer to my next sabbatical." He said it with a smile on his face, and he loves his work, so I interpreted his words as exuberance over sabbaticals more than cynicism about the daily life of college professors. And he is quite right—sabbaticals are an amazing privilege for those of us afforded the opportunity.

On my last sabbatical, my wife, Lisa, and I took our laptop computers and headed out to various places throughout the world to read, reflect and write. (Lisa is also an academic and was on sabbatical at the time.) My project was a general book, published in 2004 as *Why Sin Matters.* Despite the title, it was a book about grace as much as it was about sin. At the time, I thought of it as my most important book: what could be more important for the living of our fragile lives than an understanding of sin and grace? Though the book was reviewed favorably—and was named as a finalist for the 2005 Evangelical Christian Publishers Association's Gold Medallion Award in the Theology/Doctrine category—the swirling winds of trade book sales are spurious and unpredictable. Before I knew it the book was languishing in the bookstores and destined to soon be out of print. Perhaps the orange cover looked too much like fire and brimstone.

Though my brief misadventure into general book publishing taught me to stay in the more stable and predictable world of authoring academic books, I was not ready to give up on the topic of sin and grace. It seems terribly important for Christians to understand these doctrines and their implications for daily living. So several years later I have tried again, writing this book about sin and grace for Christian counselors, seminarians, psychology students, pastors and others with an interest in soul care. There are a few strategic passages adapted from *Why Sin Matters,* but for the most part, it is a fresh look at a topic I have been considering for several years now.

Somewhere along the journey of being raised evangelical, and then staying in the evangelical church as an adult, I picked up a view of sin and grace that was quite forensic in nature. That is, sin is a violation of God's moral will, and grace is God's decision to forgive our sins through the life and work of Jesus. I still hold to this view, but I am gaining new appreciation for the relational context of the Christian story. It's not that God comes up with arbitrary rules and then rewards or punishes us based on our compliance. Rather, God is relational, and created us to be relational. The tragedy of sin is the breaking of our relationships with God and one another. But God, whose character and purposes have always been relational, has redeemed and is redeeming us through the grace revealed in Jesus Christ. There is a forensic dimension to this, of course, but the power of God's love is the most remarkable part of the Christian narrative. In grace, God desires to sanctify us so that we become more and more like the only fully functioning human who ever lived. And as we become more like Jesus, our counseling cannot help but be transformed by the grace that brings such renewal and hope.

This book is an exploration of how Christian views of sin and grace relate to Christian counseling. In the first chapter I consider the gulf between biblical counselors and Christian psychologists, which is often expressed as a disagreement about how one should handle sin when working with clients. It seems to me that much of this disagreement reflects a misunderstanding of biblical counseling and the inseparability of the Christian doctrines of sin and grace. Chapter two is a look at sin from an Augustinian perspective. I argue that an Augustinian view of sin ought to be a source of empathy for Christian counselors because we are all in this mess together. The depth of God's grace (both common and special grace) is considered in chapter three. If counseling is a process of *dis*covery and *re*covery, then grace is essential to help clients experience enough safety to explore the hidden places of their lives. Chapter four provides three vantage points for the importance of holding sin and grace together: psychology, theology and spirituality. The final four chapters of the book consider sin and grace from the perspective of *Integrative Psychotherapy*—a multidimensional approach to counseling that Clark Campbell and I recently described in another IVP Academic book. *Integrative Psychotherapy* posits three domains of intervention: functional, structural and relational. Each of these is related to a particular aspect of the image of God, so each of them also involves particular nuances for how we understand sin and grace in Christian counseling.

Christian counselors have divided over the doctrines of sin and grace, which is both sad and unnecessary. I hope this small book will prompt us to look again at the central themes of the Christian faith and consider how doctrine informs the soul care we provide. How freeing a sound doctrine of sin can be, because it ushers us into the presence of a surprising grace that touches our deepest spiritual and psychological longings.

1

Divided by Sin

SOMETIMES THE CLEAREST DIVISIONS IN LIFE do not hold up well under scrutiny. In my case, I once divided Christian counseling into two distinct categories: the biblical counselors and the integrationists. On one hand, biblical counselors were—more or less—the bad guys. Trained in conservative seminaries and influenced by writers like Jay Adams, they had one goal in therapy: to root out sin in their clients' lives. They did not know much about psychology, and they seemed insensitive to relational aspects of counseling. I, on the other hand, was a good guy—an integrationist. Trained as a clinical psychologist at a reputable university, I understood a good deal about psychology and still affirmed the importance of theological orthodoxy. My approach to psychotherapy, I thought, was more sophisticated and nuanced than the biblical counselors'. The division was clear in my mind: they emphasized sin, I emphasized grace.

Philip Monroe messed up my tidy categorization of Christian counseling. Phil and I first met in my office at Wheaton College when I was interviewing him for the doctoral program in clinical psychology that I was directing at the time. Phil was an unusual candidate because he was coming from the "other side." Trained at Westminster Seminary in biblical counseling, he wanted a graduate degree in psychology also. Before the interview, I was expecting not to recommend him for admission; after all, he was one of *them*. But to my surprise, I found him a delightful, engaging, compassionate man. I was drawn to his love of theology and people. We accepted Phil into our program, and he came and studied at Wheaton College for five years. I suspect I learned at least as much from Phil during that half-decade as he learned from me. He helped me get beyond my caricatures and misunderstandings of biblical counseling and helped me to see the importance of a theological perspective on counseling. While in our graduate program, Phil wrote an article in *Journal of Psychology and Theology* about building bridges between biblical counselors and Christian psychologists (Monroe, 1997). Now he is a licensed psychologist teaching at Biblical Seminary where he is still building bridges. Though my audience for this book is mostly intended for those in the integrationist tradition, I hope it helps build some bridges also.

Seemingly, the doctrine of sin has become a watershed among Christian counselors. On one side of the divide are the many seminarians, pastors and biblical counselors who identify themselves with biblical counseling (Powlison, 2000, 2001) or nouthetic counseling (Adams, 1970). On the other side, many pastoral counselors, Christian psychologists, social workers and psychotherapists prefer to emphasize the integration of faith and the behavioral sciences. The dividing line has been drawn, and loyalties run deep. Counselors in one group attend conferences of the Christian Counseling and Educational Foundation (www.ccef.org) and subscribe to *The Journal of Biblical Counseling*. Counselors in the other group attend the Christian Association for Psychological Studies (www.caps.net) and subscribe to *The Journal of Psychology and Christianity*. Educational institutions have joined one side or the other—some offering degrees in biblical counseling and others degrees in Christian counseling or clinical psychology. Churches have entered the fray. Some embrace contemporary psychological methods; others insist that all psychology must be rejected. And many practitioners first identify what they do *not* believe (I am *not* a biblical counselor, or I am *not* an integrationist) even before they identify what they *do* believe. But could it be that these divisions over the doctrine of sin reflect some deeper divide about the nature of what it means to be human and how we relate to a God who longs to draw us close in loving relationship?

If the watershed is about the doctrines of sin and grace—with some Christian counselors emphasizing sin while others emphasize grace—then it is not surprising that most choose grace. Shall I emphasize sin with my clients, causing them to slink further into shame and remorse for their struggles and perhaps take on unnecessary guilt for events over which they have no control? Or shall I emphasize grace, accepting my clients as Christ has accepted me, allowing them to grow into awareness of their strengths and weaknesses? Stated this way, the choice is clear. Who wouldn't choose grace?

But maybe the matter is not so simple. Dividing the Christian counseling world into a sin camp and a grace camp is misleading and incorrect. I suggest this for two reasons. First, the biblical counseling movement is not pri-

---

COUNSELING TIP 1.1: *The Confirmation Bias Affects Counselors Too*

Cognitive psychologists write about the confirmation bias, which means that people seek out information consistent with what they already believe and avoid contrary information. Consider how this might work for Mandy, a newly graduated Christian psychologist or counselor who has heard negative things about the biblical counseling movement. Rather than reading what biblical counselors are actually saying, Mandy might be content to read those who criticize biblical counseling. She will be confirming what she already believes, which helps her simplify the world and make sense of her counseling methods. But notice that she may also be quite wrong because she has never read the *Journal of Biblical Counseling* or a book by a convinced biblical counselor. She might become a much better Christian counselor after reading some of the biblical counseling materials. Even if she disagrees sharply with what the biblical counselors have to say, at least she will be in a position to consider perspectives that she had not considered before.

---

marily about sin. The critics of the movement reduce biblical counselors to counselors who hold naive and simplistic views of sin, often without even reading their work. More accurately, the biblical counseling movement is primarily about Christian anthropology and ecclesiology. They are trying to reclaim a Christian view of health and functioning that keeps the care of souls within the ministries and teachings of the church. The doctrine of sin is a key Christian teaching, of course, so it is one of several tenets emphasized by biblical counselors. Psychology is viewed skeptically by biblical counselors because it has removed the care of souls from the ministry of the church, and because it has supplanted a Christian view of persons with a subtle and pernicious tug toward a secular view of human functioning. Dividing the Christian counseling world into a sin camp and a grace camp, and then associating biblical counselors with the sin camp, does terrible injustice to what they are saying.

Second, it is not helpful to divide Christian counselors according to sin and grace because it distorts Christian doctrine. Sin and grace may warrant separate chapters in a systematic theology text, because both are huge concepts and we must divide books into chapters somehow, but the concepts are so deeply and thoroughly interconnected that one cannot possibly be understood without the other; grace cannot be understood without understanding the extent of our sin, and we must have the hope of grace in order to look honestly at the depth of our sin. When Christian counselors attempt to emphasize sin without grace, or grace without sin, they distort both.

The Lost Language of Sin and Grace

There was once a time when the language of sin and grace was understood, both in private and public discourse, but that era has largely been supplanted by a therapeutic culture that emphasizes symptoms more than sin and unconditional acceptance more than grace. The language of sin has been replaced with a language of crime and sickness (Menninger, 1973; Taylor, 2000). One leading psychologist even suggested that the belief in sin is what makes people disturbed (Ellis, 1960, 1971), though he has recently recanted this belief (Ellis, 2000).

I sometimes read Puritan prayers to my students, and then we pause to ponder what sort of response such a prayer might engender in churches today. For example, consider these two phrases from separate prayers:

> It is fitting thou shouldest not regard me,
> for I am vile and selfish;
> yet I seek thee,
> and when I find thee there is no wrath
> to devour me,
> but only sweet love. (Bennett, 1975, p. 46)

> No poor creature stands in need of divine grace more than I do,
> And yet none abuses it more than I have done, and still do.
> How heartless and dull I am!
> Humble me in the dust for not loving thee more.
> Every time I exercise any grace renewedly
> I am renewedly indebted to thee,
> the God of all grace, for special assistance. (Bennett, 1975, p. 111)

Imagine how public prayers such as these might be perceived today. The person offering such a prayer might be prescribed a selective serotonin reuptake inhibitor (e.g., Prozac), sent to a pastoral counselor or referred to a self-esteem group. The language of sin seems quaint, a relic of some old-time religion, and though the word *grace* has persisted, it cannot possibly mean the same thing as it did before we lost track of sin.

Today we use *grace* as a synonym for being lenient or tolerant: "I will show some grace and accept late papers," or "You have a ten-day grace period by which to make your mortgage payment." This is a shallow, vapid, consumerist sort of grace compared to what was known in previous generations when people went trembling into the confessional booth and emerged with the lightness of step that comes with forgiveness of sin.

The Puritan prayers may seem harsh or old-fashioned, but they remind us of how far sin separates us from God and how desperately we need a solution so that we can be ushered back into relationship with God—a God who has demonstrated a passionate and holy love for humanity from the Garden of Eden until today. The doctrines of sin and grace are ultimately our great hope because they reverberate with some primordial rhythm in the human soul, giving us the courage to believe in a God who is restoring and redeeming all creation.

In his book *Whatever Became of Sin?* Karl Menninger, a distinguished twentieth-century psychiatrist, describes his eyewitness account of how sin disappeared. "When I was a boy, sin was still a serious matter and the word was not a jocular term. But I saw this change; I saw it go. I am afraid I even joined in hailing its going" (Menninger, 1973, p. 24). Menninger goes on to describe a new social morality, which was introduced with contemporary mental health research and practice; psychiatrists and psychologists became the high priests of this new moral order. While Menninger affirms the importance of mental health professions, he regrets that the concept of sin did not survive the transition. I would add that a true understanding of grace has also been lost, because it cannot exist without a language of sin.

And now we can see what the biblical counselors are saying. They are not saying we should call our clients sinners and demand repentance in the counseling office as much as they are calling us back to a way of thinking that is easily lost in today's flurry of mental health activity. A theological worldview has been supplanted by a therapeutic paradigm as one vocabulary has been traded in for another. In the process we may have lost our understanding of what it means to be fallen humans in God's world.

Jennifer was a bright young woman, newly married, trying desperately to recover from that awful Wednesday evening. Finances were tight, as they often are for newlyweds, so Jennifer took a job at the local convenience store. She stepped away from the counter one evening to get something from the back room when she realized that a customer had followed her. The next moments were a horrifying haze of knife-point threats, partial disrobing, the foul stench of unwanted closeness and, ultimately, forced sexual penetration. When the rapist was satisfied, he holstered his knife and walked out the front door as if he had bought a pack of chewing gum or cigarettes. Meanwhile Jennifer lay sobbing beside cases of beer in the back room, forever changed.

In our counseling, Jennifer and I needed the language of sin. She needed a word like sin to understand what had happened. How else could such horror be understood? Her perpetrator had not merely made a mistake. This was not just a bad choice. His behavior was not merely a symptom of some psychological disorder. This was horrendous sin, and it needed to be named and grieved, over and over. We needed the language of sin to exonerate her. This was not her doing. It was not her sin. She was targeted, stalked and devastated by the sin of another. And she needed a caring, gentle listener to help her walk back into memories of the trauma, to help her weep and lament and try to make sense of her future.

This may seem like an easy clinical example because it identifies a sin done *to* the client rather than *by* the client. Who wouldn't view rape as a horrendous offense worthy of the label of sin? But what does a Christian counselor do when a client is struggling with a personal pattern of sin? Here again, the temptation is to bifurcate the world into two artificial categories— those who are sinned against and those who are sinning themselves. As I will explore further in chapter two, this is a misleading and simplistic view of sin. Even in Jennifer's case, where the source of the problem was so clearly a sin against her, she found it had devastating implications in her own personal choices thereafter.

Events like rape change people. In the months following, Jennifer found herself irritable, aloof and annoyed easily by her husband. She screamed out in rage and anxiety, but the rapist who caused her pain was not there to hear, so her feelings spilled over onto undeserving loved ones. Her relationships became strained, her emotions frazzled, her hope compromised.

Here we see the complexity of sin. It is not merely packaged inside the skin of a single human being. We are social beings, constantly interacting with one another, always being influenced by the sin of the world around us. Jennifer had been violated, and though she had no culpability for this tragic rape, the rape cost her so dearly that it submerged her into a pattern

IN THE OFFICE 1.1: Whispering the Language of Sin

Considering sin in therapy does not mean that a counselor calls a client a sinner. The following counseling dialogue reveals a gentle acknowledgment of sin, struggle and a cry for grace without ever using the word *sin*.

Jennifer: Things were rough this week with Justin. I know he just wants to help, but sometimes he drives me crazy.

Mark: I know that has been a challenge for you lately. Tell me more about him driving you crazy.

Jennifer: He's just always asking stuff, like if I'm okay or if I had any dreams last night or if I would favor the death penalty for rape. It's just nonstop. And I ask him to stop, and he does for a few days, and then he starts all over again.

Mark: Yeah, and it really gets to you.

Jennifer: Completely. I'm so annoyed.

Mark: How does your feeling annoyed come out in your relationship with Justin?

Jennifer: I don't think I treat him very well. Sometimes I just get really frustrated and scream at him. He looks really hurt and walks away, and I feel terrible.

Mark: That's not how you want to respond.

Jennifer: No, not at all. I feel terrible about it.

Mark: Yes, I see that, both in your words and in your eyes.

Jennifer: [crying] I need to handle this better. I just feel all tied up inside, like any little thing sets me off. I'm so tense and upset and afraid.

Mark: You're trying to move on, but it feels tougher than you could have imagined.

Jennifer: Yes, and I'm so tired and confused too.

The client and counselor are whispering a language of sin and grace, even without using the words.

of sinful and damaging interactions with family members. With time and ample doses of grace from God, caring friends, family members and her therapist, Jennifer was able to grieve her loss, recover the majority of her hope, renew strained relationships and move ahead with life.

It seems to me that Christian psychotherapists and biblical counselors might handle someone like Jennifer in similar ways. Both would sit with her in her pain, listen to her story, and allow her to grieve, weep and ask the sort of questions that injured people ask. Both would identify the rapist's behavior as an evil, horrendous act—a rupture of human civility. Both would notice that Jennifer herself began treating people unkindly in the aftermath of the rape, and whether or not they used the word *sin* they would be concerned about helping Jennifer reclaim an ability to treat her friends and family better. Biblical counselors might use a theological vocabulary in understanding Jennifer while Christian psychotherapists use a psychological vocabulary—and these different vocabularies are no small matter—but ultimately both are likely to provide competent care for a hurting person.

Transcending the Divide

As an integrationist, I believe there is value in both psychology and Christian theology. We ought to study and learn about human nature—however fallen it has become—and psychology helps us do so with its various theories, scientific findings and methods. But let us not slip into the trap of thinking that we are offering grace while the biblical counselors are preaching about sin. Too often we integrationists are minimizing both grace and sin because our psychological vocabulary does not allow for these notions. Here we have a good deal to learn from the biblical counselors and the theological tradition they represent.

In losing track of sin, we have also lost a careful theological definition of our most basic human problem. For some, the word *sin* evokes images of angry fundamentalist preachers who seem more intent on condemning and judging than searching for forgiveness and grace. Others think of *sin* as a word used to manipulate and coerce people into particular ways of behavior. Still others think of sin lightly, as a topic of lighthearted joking or a name for a city where people go to gamble and party (that one can buy a motorcycle at a place called Sin City Scooters in Las Vegas is evidence of how imprecisely and lightly we have come to view sin). Only as we move beyond these distorted views of sin can we reclaim it as part of an essential vocabulary—one that opens the possibility of forgiveness, redemption, and renewed relationships with God and others.

From a Christian perspective, sin is failing to conform to God's moral law (Erickson, 1985). Sin is evident both in our fallen state (i.e., our distorted dispositions) and in our actions. It is both personal and corporate. It is both forensic—meaning that we have violated God's will—and relational, causing a tragic distance between humanity and our loving Creator. In an earlier book, which I mentioned in the introduction to this one, Clark Campbell and I presented a model for Christian counseling that is based on three views of what it means to be made in the image of God (McMinn & Campbell, 2007). These same three views of the *imago Dei*—functional, structural and relational—are helpful in understanding the nature of sin and our desperate need for grace.

From a functional perspective, God created humans and instructed them to manage themselves and creation with goodness and self-control. We have fallen short. Wars divide our world, pollution produced for the sake of convenience and profit threatens the health of creation, and our failures of self-control are evident everywhere—in crime, addiction, poverty, pornography, violence, gluttony, consumerism and so much more.

From a structural vantage point, God created humans with certain ontological capacities, to speak and reason and understand morality. These capacities have been compromised by original sin. (Original sin refers to the state into which we are born as opposed to the sinful choices we voluntarily make later in life.) As King David cried out in Psalm 51:5, "For I was born a sinner— / yes, from the moment my mother conceived me," so also, centuries later, Augustine reflected: "For in your sight, no one is free from sin, not even the infant whose life is but a day upon the earth" (Augustine 398/1986, p. 7). Because of this sinful nature, our God-given structural capacities are weakened and distorted. Our capacity to think well, to determine the moral alternative, to understand the complexities of the created order have all been tainted by our sinful nature. Our human will has become corrupted and twisted, even before we consciously chose sin, so that we do not naturally love God first and neighbor as self.

Only God, in grace, can break through our blindness and offer us salvation. Relational views of the *imago Dei* emphasize that God's character is seen in the relationships humans form with one another and with God. God's purposes, which arise from God's character, are revealed in relationship with humanity. It is not so much that any individual contains an ontological stamp bearing God's nature, but that our relating to God and one another is a reflection of a God who cares so much about relationship that he sent Jesus to reestablish a covenantal relationship with lost hu-

manity. Here again, we see the devastating consequences of sin. Our relationships have been damaged—both our relationships with other humans and our relationship with God. Conflict is all around us, ranging
from interpersonal to international, and we have turned away from God—
the source of greatest joy—in our relentless quest for personal fulfillment
and pleasure.

In all these ways we see the wreckage of sin extending through all creation, but this is not the end of the gospel. Indeed, it is a starting point for
understanding the incredible grace God extends. The apostle Paul describes
how human sin makes the good news so vivid. "God's law was given so that
all people could see how sinful they were. But as people sinned more and
more, God's wonderful grace became more abundant. So just as sin ruled
over all people and brought them to death, now God's wonderful grace
rules instead, giving us right standing with God and resulting in eternal life
through Jesus Christ our Lord" (Rom 5:20-21). God's grace is both justifying
and sanctifying. Grace justifies those who accept Christ's gift of salvation, re-
generating us and making us pure in God's sight. "As a result, he has
brought you into his own presence, and you are holy and blameless as you
stand before him without a single fault" (Col 1:22). And grace is also sanctifying, sticking with us over time, causing us to be transformed into the
women and men God desires us to be.

Sin is offensive and unpopular. Grace is winsome and inviting. If given a
choice, we should all choose grace. But we cannot approach sin and grace
as separate items on a menu; Christian theology will simply not allow it. As
will be explored in subsequent chapters, we cannot possibly understand the
Christian doctrine of grace unless we understand sin.

It is a curious thing that those of us involved in the integration movement
have not studied and written about sin very much. We are interested in human behavior and theology, so would it not seem reasonable for us to study
the meaning and implications of sin alongside our interest in grace? After all,
sin is a central doctrine of the Christian faith, and the problems and consequences of human evil are continually confronted in the therapy office.
When Philip Monroe (2001) looked for articles about sin in the integration
literature he found almost nothing, and most of what has been written has
been an effort to view sin through the lens of various psychological theories.
Monroe concludes:

> No matter what the therapist's theoretical orientation is, therapy will deal with

SURVEY SAYS 1.1: Sin Matters

With the help of four graduate students, I surveyed a sample of Christian leaders in 2005, asking them, "What do you wish every psychologist knew about the nature of sin?" The survey went out to pastors, theologians, biblical scholars, missionaries and ministry leaders. In all, 171 Christian leaders replied to the question. My students and I organized the answers we received and wrote a brief research article for a journal published by the American Psychological Association (McMinn, Ruiz, Marx, Wright & Gilbert, 2006). We sifted through a number of wise and helpful comments in the process. For example:

> I wish all of us—pastors and psychologists alike—were more realistic about sin . . . its pervasiveness, it's blinding effect upon us, its persistence in us. We need to communicate without apology that human beings are capable of enormous evil and of enormous good. Both sides of the truth need to come through.
>
> To me, this is the crux of clinical counseling. Is the problem a consequence of sinful choices or of a psychological or neurological disorder? Sin should not be the cause of every disorder. Neither should it be dismissed or minimized as a root cause either.
>
> One can deal with the topic of sin in a compassionate manner in therapy that is not shameful. Most psychologists I know associate discussions of sin automatically with shame.

I will draw on the wisdom of these Christian leaders throughout this book. They have much insight to offer, and many have concerns about the ways Christian psychologists have avoided talking about sin.

the sins of clients. But the dominant culture that sets boundaries for appropriate care of persons does not generally consider sinfulness and all of its ramifications as a significant influence on human functioning and behavior. Because we function within the dominant paradigm, we also may be tempted to downplay the effect of sin in our clients' lives, or at least to remove the traditional vocabulary of sin. It is my belief that we must consider the result of the vocabulary we use when we talk about sin. In our effort to contextualize our message to clients, we often use words that are more palatable. . . . However, does our new vocabulary cause the concept of sin to lose its . . . meaning because sin's devastation and Godward orientation are softened? Does the vocabulary of shortcomings and dysfunction direct our eyes away from the destructiveness of sin and God's holiness? Does our vocabulary encourage a lifestyle of self-examination and repentance? (p. 217)

Monroe provides an important corrective for those of us involved in integration. The language of sin is important in the contemporary and historic witness of the church, in the lives of individuals and communities, and in the Christian counseling office.

I became convinced of this when I was asked to deliver a plenary address to the Christian Association of Psychological Studies in 2002. The theme of the conference was "Grace, Freedom, and Responsibility." As I began preparing for my talk, looking into the psychological and theological literature on grace, I realized how little can be said about grace without also attending to sin. Eventually I decided to title my talk, which was scheduled for the first night of the conference, "Prelude to Grace: A Psychology of Sin and a Sin of Psychology." The premise of that talk, and of this book, is that we Christian psychologists have been remiss in considering sin. We are right to be so attracted to grace, but how much deeper and richer our understanding of grace can be if we reclaim a Christian view of sin.

Amazing Grace

Amazing grace, how sweet the sound . . . There was a time when I would sing out the first phrase of John Newton's beloved hymn but then—convinced I was no wretch—sit in rebellious silence for the next six words. I was a young man back then, just finished with a doctoral program in clinical psychology and filled with some shallow version of self-esteem I had learned in the process, crossing the threshold of adulthood with great confidence in human potential. I was wrong.

Back in those days of youthful arrogance, I wrote a book about grace. The book was never published. I sent my two-hundred-fifty-page manuscript to several different publishers, and each of them responded with a permutation of the standard "thanks, but no thanks" letter. Twenty years later, I am grateful that book was never published. It was a book produced by an overachieving, young, assistant professor who wasn't ready to write about grace. It was written before I began to grasp the depth of brokenness and sin and lostness in our world and in my own heart. Understanding grace cannot be done without understanding sin. Sometimes I ponder what that unpublished book, with its anemic view of grace, would have been titled if it had been published. Perhaps *Grace Lite* or *Grace: Because I'm Worth It* or

Grace: I'm Good Enough, I'm Smart Enough and, Doggonit, People Like Me.

Like many Christian counselors in our therapeutic culture, I sometimes try to muster amazement about grace without taking sin seriously, searching for the beauty of Easter without the ashes of Lent, insisting I am found before admitting how lost I sometimes get. Sin and grace are part of the same story, and if we leave out either part, we end up with a shallow, life-draining theology and psychology.

Newton himself lived and told a story of sin and grace. I have often heard Christians speak of his powerful story: how Newton was once a slave trader who was gripped by God's love in the midst of a tumultuous storm on the high seas. But his story is not as simple as the one we tend to tell in our churches. Here is the way we tend to tell the story: Newton grew up in a culture in which slavery was commonplace and ended up lured by avarice into the slave-trading business. But then, during an awful storm in March of 1748, he saw the wretchedness of his greed and was sickened by his crimes against humanity. *I once was lost but now am found.* From that moment forward Newton turned against slavery, devoted himself to God and became a tireless crusader against the horrendous social evil of slavery. This is the sanitized version of Newton's life that we often hear from pulpits and read on Christian web sites. But it is not true.

I wish each of our life stories, and the stories of our clients, could be neat and tidy: we are lost in our sin, but then we find God—or, more correctly, God finds us—and we bask in the light of being found as we live happily ever after. All our troubles melt away, our priorities seem clear, our strained relationships are suddenly healed, we cast off our sins and self-deceptions, and we settle into a life of faithful obedience to God. Despite my best wishes, this was not Newton's story. It's not my story either, and it is not the story of my counseling clients.

It is true that Newton had some sort of awakening from a shockingly profane and blasphemous existence as he guided the *Greyhound*—a ship that carried gold, ivory and beeswax (rather than slaves)—through mountainous ocean swells. Before Newton's devout mother died, when he was six, she had instilled in him some knowledge of God, and in these hours of almost certain death, Newton returned to the faith of his youth. His blind eyes may have been opened on that dismal March night, but not wide enough to see the full extent of his lostness and his culture's evil. The ship drifted for several weeks before finding the coast of Northern Ireland. Newton stayed in

Londonderry for six weeks as the ship was being repaired, attending prayer services, studying the Christian faith and renouncing his former way of life. He later reflected:

> I was no longer an infidel; I heartily renounced my former profaneness; I had taken up some right notions, was seriously disposed, and sincerely touched with a sense of the undeserving mercy I had received in being brought safely through so many dangers. I was sorry for my past misspent life, and purposed an immediate reformation . . . yet still I was greatly deficient in many respects. . . . I was little aware of the innate evils of my heart. (Martin, 1950, p. 79)

Upon Newton's return to Liverpool he promptly signed on as mate of the *Brownlow,* a ship that sailed to Africa, where Newton relapsed into a life of sexual sin despite his commitment to Mary Catlett, his wife to be. He later described himself as a dog returning to his vomit. These were obvious sins to Newton, arousing guilt and a desire to live better. But far more alarming was the abhorrent sin and disordered passions he could not see because his culture blinded him from the truth. The *Brownlow* docked in the Sierra Leone River as Newton traveled from village to village buying slaves and returning them as cargo to the ship. He then sailed across the Atlantic, studying a Latin Bible in his quarters as two hundred slaves lay in the hull, shackled two by two, squeezed into shelves like secondhand books. As many as a third died during the long voyage across the ocean, and many more suffered serious illnesses. When the ship arrived in Charleston, South Carolina, Newton's crew sold the slaves into a life of toil and oppression as he sat in church services and took leisurely strolls through fields and woods outside Charleston.

Like Newton, we view our lives through the lens of self-interest. We so naturally elevate our selves, families and communities above others and uncritically accept the social evils we perpetuate. Newton had little concept of slavery being wrong—few Christians of his day did. Sometimes I wonder how blind I am, how blind each of us are, to the cultural deceptions of our times. What lingering oppression of slavery remains, and how have I blinded myself to the evils of institutional racism? How has a global economy helped me, living in a country that consumes most of the world's resources, while hurting others in less fortunate circumstances? What other sins skulk in my soul, yet I am without the awareness or language to name them, let alone change them?

While Newton was in Charleston—a city influenced by George White-

---

COUNSELING TIP 1.2: *Seeing Is Believing, or Is It the Other Way Around?*

The human capacity for self-deception is mind-boggling. Though we may assume that seeing something makes us believe it, a good deal of social science evidence suggests it is the other way around; what we believe shapes what we are able to see. John Newton's story illustrates how the cultural norms of his day so completely shaped his perceptions that he studied his Latin Bible happily even as he was stealing and selling human lives. He truly was blind to his sin. Though the cultural issues are different today, we are still vulnerable to the same processes of self-deception.

Perhaps a client is justifying a bitter attitude or a decision to behave contrary to Christian morality or excusing a past failure. When a client seems to be self-deceiving, here are some questions and prompts that can be useful:

- "I have the sense that you're trying to convince yourself that you made the right decision."

- "Is there any other way you could look at this situation?"

- "What do others who know you well have to say about this?"

- "How does this decision fit with your faith commitments?"

- "Who is a person you trust, maybe someone in your faith community, who could give you another perspective on this?"

---

field's preaching on civility to slaves—the slave trader began writing letters and journal entries that showed pity for his human cargo. God was working in Newton's heart, but still he resisted. Newton returned to England, married Mary Catlett and then squandered his money on the lottery before embarking on another slave-trading journey—this time as captain of the *Duke of Argyle*. More than a year later he returned home, having purchased and sold another two hundred human lives, and read extensively on the Christian faith during his time ashore. Still he did not stop.

He captained another ship, the *African,* on yet more slave voyages. Newton became a pastor to his crews, helping them see the grace of God, as his eyes remained mostly closed to the plight of the slaves the ship carried. The conditions of capture and transport were horrendous. Though more humane than most slave-ship captains, at times Newton resorted to torturing slaves to quell insurrections. Yet he wrote how being the captain of a slave ship was optimal for "promoting the Life of God in the Soul." He could exert some control over the behavior of his crew, had ample leisure time for studying, was removed from temptations to waste time in social engagements and could observe the majesty of God's creation. He regularly saw God deliver him from hazards of death.

Newton's slave trading might have continued for many more years except for a seizure that made a career change medically necessary. In all, Newton spent ten years trading slaves, most of them *after* reclaiming his Christian faith. Newton's real life story is not the sanitized version we often hear, yet it is hauntingly familiar to the Christian journey we see in ourselves. Our disordered passions do not suddenly become ordered with a flash of insight or a spiritual awakening. Change is a lifelong calling, an epic journey. It was not until many years later that Newton could write, "I once was lost but now am found." He could write about amazing grace only as he began to see the depth of his sin.

How lost we all can be. So many prideful sins lurk beneath our awareness, stealing away the abundant life God desires for us and those around us. But God does not give up. "And I am certain that God, who began the good work within you, will continue his work until it is finally finished on the day when Christ Jesus comes back again" (Phil 1:6).

Newton became a customs officer, studied theology and, eventually—despite feelings of unworthiness because of his past sins—became a minister at Olney, England, where he preached as many as a dozen sermons a week and often wrote a hymn a week. He loved Mary faithfully, served his congregation and community well, and became an advocate for the abolition of slavery. Sometimes he annoyed parishioners because he seemed too gentle on sinners—perhaps because he saw the depths of sin in his past and was moved to extend mercy, as God had extended him such amazing grace. Newton believed that hearts are softened by the grace of the gospel, not by harsh accusation.

As Newton's eyes opened more fully with each passing year, he was horrified at his sin. One of his friends later recalled that he never spent thirty minutes with Newton without hearing the former captain's remorse for trading slaves. It was always on his mind, nagging his conscience while reminding him of his utter dependence on God's forgiving grace. John Newton's pamphlet, *Thoughts upon the African Slave Trade,* played an important role in the political battles to end slave trade. Two months before Newton's seventy-ninth birthday, after a major political victory for abolition, he wrote to a friend in Parliament: "Though I can scarcely see the paper before me I must attempt to express my thankfulness to the Lord, and to offer my congratulations to you for . . . your unwearied endeavours for the abolition of the slave trade, which I have considered as a millstone, sufficient, of itself sufficient, to sink such an enlightened and highly favour'd nation as ours to the bottom of the sea" (Martin, 1950, p. 355).

When I began reading about Newton, I expected sudden enlightenment to come with his faith conversion on the stormy North Atlantic. I hoped the lostness of his heart would suddenly be reversed, allowing him to love God and others above himself. How foolish my expectation! Sometimes I demand the same from myself and those I counsel: that our sin should suddenly be solved by a moment of insight, a spiritual renewal or a commitment to change. How wrong this is. We are broken souls, struggling to see more clearly as God continues to work in our lives. Sight is a long process, calling us to a "long obedience" (Peterson, 1980).

Seeing ourselves clearly occurs over a lifetime of pursuing God. Our vision is seldom restored in a single burst of light but with countless rays streaming into our darkened eyes over many years—and always in the midst of amazing grace. At the end of his life Newton said to his friends, "My memory is nearly gone; but I remember two things: That I am a great sinner, and that Christ is a great Savior" (Christian History Institute, 2004).

I am the guy who used to sit in church refusing to sing the second phrase of "Amazing Grace": that saved a wretch like me. But with the passing years I have begun to see what John Newton eventually saw in his life—that being amazed by grace also requires being honest about the sin that resides deep in one's character. Our greatest faults are often the ones we cannot see, and our supreme hope is found in a God who loves us despite our sin, calls us back into loving relationship, and helps us grow toward greater awareness and holiness. God's love is deeper and richer and more abundant than I ever imagined as a young man. *Amazing grace, how sweet the sound, that saved a wretch like me.* I sing it out.

Karl Menninger, though theologically unorthodox from my evangelical vantage point, seems to have come to a similar conclusion in *Whatever Became of Sin?* Menninger (1973) concludes: "Preach! Tell it like it is. Say it from the pulpit. Cry it from the housetops. What shall we cry? Cry comfort, cry repentance, cry hope. Because recognition of our part in the world transgression is the only remaining hope" (p. 228). Likewise, in her fine book *Speaking of Sin,* Barbara Brown Taylor—college professor and Episcopal priest—suggests that "sin is our only hope" because it calls us back to a theological vocabulary that causes us to place ourselves in the merciful hands of God (Taylor, 2000, p. 41).

It is unlikely that Christian psychologists and biblical counselors will ever agree on all counseling methods and theoretical matters—there are simply too many epistemological differences to expect complete rapprochement. But we can learn to listen to one another and to engage in dialogue characterized by some portion of the grace and truth revealed in Christ (Jn 1:14). As we learn from one another we can transcend the naïve bifurcation that suggests one group is interested in sin and the other in grace. These doctrines must be held together, for the doctrine of sin holds the hope of amazing grace for Christian counselors and their clients.

2

The Weight of Sin

HAVING TAUGHT CLINICAL PSYCHOLOGY DOCTORAL STUDENTS at Christian colleges for almost two decades now, I have heard the same complaint countless times: "I take my theology classes because they are required, but I can't figure out what they have to do with the practice of psychology." Though I sometimes battle a primitive impulse to blame my students for their naiveté in even making such a statement, in my better moments I realize that they are voicing a legitimate concern. Theology ought to have psychological implications, and if it doesn't we have failed to sufficiently root our psychology in matters of faith or to explore the practical meaning of Christian theology. Effective integration ought to engage both psychology and theology.

An illustration of this mutual engagement is seen in the Christian doctrine of sin and the psychological construct of empathy. A comprehensive view of sin emphasizes the human condition of sin, sinful personal choices and the consequences of sin (both the consequences of our personal sin and the consequences of others' sin). This sort of large view not only helps counselors experience empathy for their clients but also helps clients experience empathy for others. This is an important goal in counseling: to help people move out of shame-based self-focus toward a more compassionate and complete view of self and others.

From the first days of graduate training, students are taught about the central role of empathy in counseling, and rightly so. Regardless of one's theoretical orientation—be it cognitive-behavioral or object relations or family systems or any other approach to therapy—empathy and other relational factors play a central role in effective counseling (Lambert & Barley, 2002). I tell my students there are three building blocks for establishing effective empathy in Christian counseling. Two of the three they would hear about in any graduate program, but the third—a sound theology of sin—is unique to a Christian view of persons (see figure 2.1).

The Doctrine of Sin Can Promote Empathy

The first building block involves the skills of empathy that every first-year graduate student masters. Counselors learn to listen well, focus on feeling words and repeat back important phrases in order to be a caring presence in their clients' lives. And there are nonverbal ways of expressing empathy too, such as leaning forward when a client is discussing particularly difficult events or feelings.

IN THE OFFICE 2.1: Empathy Skills

Notice several empathy skills in the following example, including verbal reflections, posture and honing in on relevant feelings.

Michael: I'm really confused right now. I hate my job, my marriage isn't working, I'm going further in debt each month, and I feel terribly depressed about it all. I honestly don't know what I can do to make my life work better.

Mark: And all these bad things are converging at the same time.
          [Here I reflect back to Michael his sense of being overwhelmed by numerous misfortunes in life.]

Michael: Yes. I just feel so overwhelmed and numb and sad.

Mark: Like you're being flattened by a huge pile of stress.
          [This is another reflection, but with imagery to help capture the magnitude of what he is describing.]

Michael: Exactly. I just don't know where to turn, who to talk with or what's going to happen to me.

Mark [leaning forward]: As I listen, I get the sense you are feeling down and discouraged, but also that you're frightened. You don't know what to do.
          [This is a more advanced empathy skill, calling out a feeling that Michael has only hinted at. Notice also that I lean forward to emphasize my presence and care for him.]

Michael: [tears welling] I hope you can help me.

Empathy skills are good and important, but techniques themselves are superficial if the counselor is not also convinced of important reasons to be empathic based on shared human experience. Consider the wise, even prophetic, words of Henri J. M. Nouwen in his now-classic book *The Wounded Healer:*

> But here we must be aware of the great temptation that will face the Christian minister of the future. Everywhere Christian leaders, men and women alike, have become increasingly aware of the need for more specific training and formation. This need is realistic, and the desire for more professionalism in the ministry is understandable. But the danger is that instead of becoming free to let the spirit grow, the future minister may entangle himself in the complications of his own assumed competence and use his specialism as an excuse to avoid the much more difficult task of being compassionate. The task of the Christian leader is to bring out the best in man *[sic]* and to lead him forward to a more human community; the danger is that his skillful diagnostic eye will become more an eye for distant and detailed analysis than the eye of a compassionate partner. (1972, p. 42)

Though Nouwen is writing generally to Christian leaders, his words seem particularly appropriate to those studying Christian counseling in seminaries and at Christian colleges and universities. Skills are important, but they need to be grounded in compassion and wisdom. Thoughtful clinicians want more than empathy *skills.* They also want to understand reasons why one should be a *compassionate partner*—to use Nouwen's term—rather than simply a technician who employs skills of empathy to help another person feel and function better.

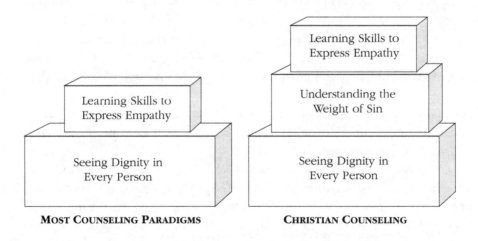

Figure 2.1. Perspectives on empathy

An important reason for empathy, positioned at the base of the two dia-grams in figure 2.1, pertains to a common belief in human worth and dig-nity. Counselors of various persuasions affirm the value of the people with whom they work. This is not unique to Christians—virtually all human ser-vice professionals assert the value of all humanity. But the reason for human worth has a distinct basis in Christianity. Christian counselors find human dignity and value in the creation story, whether they deem it to be a literal account of creation or a love poem describing the relationship of God to humanity. In creation we see God doing something magnificent with human character: "So God created people in his own image; / God patterned them after himself; / male and female he created them" (Gen 1:27). Because hu-mans are created in the image of God (the *imago Dei*), there is something to be cherished in each human person; therein lies a reflection of divine goodness. Furthermore, every human is deeply loved by God and is deserv-ing of empathy, attention, compassion and human love.

Virtually all counselors agree with these first two building blocks for em-pathy: active listening skills and a belief in human dignity. Christian coun-selors also affirm these two building blocks of empathy, but there is a third basis for empathy that is rarely considered apart from a Christian view of persons: the weight of sin.

The suggestion of sin as a basis for empathy may cause some to bristle. Speaking of sin in counseling seems adversarial, confrontational, even accu-satory, and many counselors have heard horror stories of how the concept of sin is used by some Christian counselors to belittle and shame their cli-ents. How could an awareness of sin possibly enhance empathy? The reason this is confusing is that we have failed to grasp a large picture of sin. As long as sin is a puny notion, perhaps limited to a list of behaviors to avoid, then it can never serve as an adequate basis for empathy. But when we take time to understand the magnitude of the sin problem, when we begin to realize that no one escapes its pull, then we begin to identify with our clients in their struggles and pain.

The essential theological distinction is between an Augustinian and Pela-gian view of sin. Augustine, writing around A.D. 400, argued that humans have an intrinsic sinfulness built into their character. When Adam and Eve sinned in the Garden, they not only affected their own destiny but also the destiny of all their progeny. Now we live in a state of original sin. Augustine used the Latin phrase *non posse non peccare,* which means that it is not pos-

---

SURVEY SAYS 2.1: Almost Genetic

Among the 171 Christian leaders we surveyed (the same survey mentioned in chapter 1), many of them mentioned the importance of an Augustinian perspective on sin. They did so without mentioning Augustine's name, but still his influence is evident in their comments. For example:

Sin is not merely a choice; we are predisposed to sin.

I wish that psychology as a field would begin with the premise that all humans are born with a sin nature and in a fallen state, instead of the notion that human beings are born basically good.

I wish that psychologists understood that sin is inextricably interwoven into the fabric of human existence.

[Sin] is very deep, almost genetic, and thus is only dealt with by grace.

Sin is an inherent part of human life. It is something that we constantly battle.

Many more examples could be cited. Christian leaders want Christian counselors to understand a good theology of original sin, because it has repercussions for how we understand and work with our clients.

---

sible for us not to sin. Humanity is fallen, making it impossible that any human could live a sinless life. In contrast, Pelagius—a contemporary of Augustine—taught *posse non peccare*: it is possible for us not to sin. Therefore, just as Adam and Eve were born with the capacity to choose right and wrong, so each human begins morally neutral, with the capacity to choose good or evil throughout life. The Pelagian view was deemed heretical by the early church, but it has proven a persistent heresy, echoing through the centuries. Despite the lingering influence of Pelagianism, most Christians today affirm that something is fundamentally wrong with humanity; it begins before any of us makes a conscious choice, and it can never be fully overcome this side of heaven.

An Augustinian view of sin has important implications for empathy in counseling. If we are all in a state of original sin, then we are able to understand the common human struggle that every person experiences. In a sense, we are all more similar than different, all created in the image of a flawless God but marred by the pernicious effects of original sin. As a therapist and client sit face to face, they are both "noble ruins" (to borrow a phrase from Pascal), which ought to call the therapist to a deep experience of empathy and understanding of the client's weaknesses, wounds and vulnerabilities.

The Russian novelist Aleksandr Solzhenitsyn came to this awareness in an unlikely place—he was lying in a dingy prison cell as a political prisoner in the former Soviet Republic.

> When I lay there on rotting prison straw . . . it was disclosed to me that the line separating good and evil passes not through states, nor between classes, nor between political parties either—but right through every human heart— and through all human hearts. . . . Even in the best of all hearts, there remains . . . an unprooted small corner of evil. (Solzhenitsyn, 1973/2002, p. 312)

Solzhenitsyn gained empathy for his captors as he recognized a similar capacity for evil in himself. This was only possible because Solzhenitsyn glimpsed the magnitude and ubiquity of the sin problem in our world.

Three Dimensions of Sin

We fail to grasp the extent and gravity of our sin when we see it in a single dimension, as violation of certain behavioral standards that ought to be maintained. We sometimes think that if we obey the Ten Commandments or if we at least behave better than today's infamous celebrities—the ones who are arrested or defrocked for public scandals—then sin does not really have such a strong grip on our lives. But sin is bigger and more powerful than we know. Sin engulfs us in three dimensions: *sinfulness, sins* and the *consequences of sin.*

To illustrate the three dimensions of sin, I turn to what experimental psychologists call "white noise." White noise is the obnoxious sound of static, like what you might get if you turned up the volume on your stereo and let the dial rest between radio stations. Imagine sitting in a university lab, trying to rearrange scrambled letters to solve an anagram, when loud static suddenly begins in the headphones you are required to wear. To what extent would the static interfere with your problem-solving ability? White noise may not seem that unpleasant from this description, but if it is persistent and loud enough, it can be quite distracting and annoying. Let's say that the white noise generator is connected to a toggle switch with an "on" and "off" position. The "on" position produces cacophony; the "off" renders silence.

Sometimes we fall prey to a toggle-switch view of sin: either we are sinning at this moment—the toggle switch is "on" and the noise of sin sur-

---

COUNSELING TIP 2.1: *Counseling Is Not Just Diagnosing and Rooting Out Sin*

A simplistic view of sin in counseling suggests that counselors need to help clients identify and root out core sins in their lives. Once the sins are removed, then the client will presumably feel and function better. Although this approach is not always or entirely misguided, because some psychological problems are related to harmful personal choices, it nonetheless reflects a shallow view of sin. Sin involves not only the acts we commit but also the state in which we live. A person may encounter various psychological problems—depression, anxiety and so on—not just because of personal sinful choices, but because of the fallen nature of all humanity and the consequences of others' sins. We all carry the unfortunate consequences of living outside of Eden.

---

rounds us—or we are not sinning—the toggle switch is "off" and we are living in a state of purity. Either we are violating God's commandments or we are not. Either we are gossiping or lying or stealing, or we are not. Toggle switch "on." Toggle switch "off." The simplicity of a toggle-switch view of sin is compelling, but it underestimates the power of sin.

Inherent sinfulness: The white noise is always on. An Augustinian perspective on sin suggests we live in a world where the white noise of sin is always humming. It can never be turned off completely. We are born as sinful creatures and enter a sinful world even before we have the choice to sin. This sinfulness speaks to our natural disposition, a malignant condition that influences the very fabric of creation and touches every aspect of our existence. We are all bent souls—every one of us—inclined toward both good and evil from the moment we are conceived.

Theologians call it original sin because it comes with us into life. We did not choose it, and we cannot choose to completely rid ourselves of it. Sinfulness infects both our thinking and our affections, blinding us to truth and causing our hearts to stray. We are "mired in a desperate and deplorable condition" (Plantinga, 2000, p. 267).

Theologian and seminary professor Millard Erickson writes: "Many people are unable to grasp the concept of sin. The idea of *sin* as an inner force, an inherent condition, a controlling power, is largely unknown. People today think more in terms of *sins,* that is, individual wrong acts" (1985, p. 564). Similar assertions can be found throughout the writings of Christian systematic theologians. J. I. Packer notes: "The assertion of original sin makes the point that we are . . . born with a nature enslaved to sin" (1993, p. 83). Donald Bloesch writes: "Sin, in the biblical perspective, is both an act and a state. . . . What should be borne in mind is that the bias of sin precedes the act of sin" (1978, p. 93). The white noise is always on—from the moment of birth to the moment of death—annoying us, distracting us, causing us to stumble.

Here we begin to see possibilities for how a sound doctrine of sin helps a therapist gain empathy. When working with a client who is deeply scarred by his or her own sin, or profoundly wounded by the sins of others, a therapist may ponder, "There but for the grace of God go I." This promotes a bit of empathy perhaps, but not as much as if the therapist ponders a more precise possibility: "There go I." The therapist may not have committed exactly the same sins or been wounded in the same ways as the client, but

---

COUNSELING TIP 2.2: *Sin and the Case for Medication*

It seems ironic that counselors most inclined to address sin in therapy are often least inclined to support medication for clients with depression, anxiety problems, thought disorders and other maladies. A good theology of sin reminds us that all humanity is broken, including our biology. Just as our wills and our thinking and our emotions are tainted by the effects of sin, so are serotonin levels and dopamine receptors. Medication has an important place in Christian counseling when one considers a large view of sin.

---

inherent in the doctrine of original sin is the premise that we are all broken humans slogging through life's challenges together. One person struggles in one way, and another in different ways, but we all live in a constant state of original sin. Sometimes we refer to this as being "only human," but of course we have it backward. If we were fully human—living in Eden before tumbling into sin—then life would be much richer and fuller than it is. The problem is not being only human, but being broken humans, fallen from our created state.

When my children were young, they would fall and scrape their knees, as children do. One day I realized something sad about myself. When they fell, I experienced a surge of inner anger at them for disrupting our time of playing together. At a moment when they needed my compassion and care, my first inclination was anger—providing ample evidence that my character is deeply flawed. Outwardly, I suppressed my surge of anger and showed them the care and compassion they needed. I raced to their aid, expressed sympathy and helped care for their wounds. I didn't sin outwardly when they scraped their knees, but my inner state reflected the sinfulness of my character. Each fall and each interior surge of anger reminded me that I am not quite right. Something about me is bent, wrong, distorted, crooked. Something in my character is less human than God intended. I am a sinful person even when I do not behave in sin. If we stop and listen, we can always hear the hum of the white noise, and this can promote empathy for our fellow human beings—all of whom struggle with ugly character qualities, as I do.

No human experience is completely devoid of sin. We all love people, and that love reflects the most noble and best facets of human nature. But our love is never completely pure; there is always a hint of self-interest or self-absorption. Our hearts cry for justice, and we feel indignant when we see evidence of racism, ageism, sexism and oppression, but even in the midst of our indignation—which is almost completely good—don't we also catch glimpses of a smug sense of self-righteousness or superiority, especially over those who care less about justice than we do? The white noise is always on. We have become so accustomed to it that we cannot even imagine the freedom of silence.

Thanks be to God who persistently and lovingly calls us back to Eden through justifying and sanctifying grace, back to relationship and wholeness and hope. Though we will never reach a state of completion this side of eternity, God is always at work in us and among us.

Our sinful choices: Cranking up the volume. The cascading crisis of sin begins with our state of original sinfulness, but it does not end there. In the midst of the chronic, low-level noise of our broken world, we sometimes choose evil. We commit sins. Consciously or unconsciously, we make sinful choices, and often we make the same choices over and over again! We willfully violate God's moral instruction, pulling away from God's desire for intimate relationship with us. As sinful creatures we rebel against God in our thoughts, attitudes, behaviors, volition and relationships. We do and think things we should not, and we fail to do and think the things we should. God established certain principles and purposes for living, and we violate those principles by putting ourselves first, above relationship with God and neighbor. In so doing we crank up the volume and immerse ourselves in the noise of our own sin. Though we may tend to minimize our sins by focusing on worse things that others have done, we are all sinners.

Here again, though, is the possibility for empathy; it is bound up in the virtue of humility. All of us have sinned, and so counselors should be able to understand the predicaments their clients face, even when the predicaments emerge from wrong choices and behaviors. Jeremy Taylor, the seventeenth-century Anglican clergyman, advised: "Call to mind every day some one of your foulest sins, or the most shameful of your disgraces, or your most indiscreet act, or anything that most troubled you, and apply it to the present swelling of your spirit, and it may help allay it" (Taylor, 1650/1988, p. 57). Taylor's advice runs contrary to contemporary mental health notions of positive self-talk, self-esteem and self-affirmation, but I wonder what might happen to counselors' ability to empathize if we followed Taylor's advice. We have all sinned, deliberately and accidentally, and we have all been wounded by the sins of others. Once we understand the ubiquity of sin we can sit *with* our clients rather than *above* them.

The consequences of sin: Deafened by a noisy world. Because we are sinners living in a sinful world, we are constantly surrounded by the consequences of sin. We are deafened by our own sin and the sin of others, and our sin contributes to the deafening noise others experience. If I act sinfully toward my spouse, she will experience some degree of loss and suffering as the result of my sin. The abused or abandoned child lives with consequences of another's sin for a lifetime. The child of an alcoholic parent finds the world an unpredictable and dangerous place. Some veterans are destined to wheelchairs because of the tragedies of war. Alvin Plantinga, a philosopher at the University of Notre Dame, states: "Because of our social nature, sin and its effects can be like a contagion that spreads from one to another, eventually corrupting an entire society or segment of it" (Plantinga, 2000, p. 207). Sin is costly.

It is not so difficult to see that others have hurt us with their self-interest. I once had a plumber fail to show up at a pre-arranged time because a more lucrative alternative became available. It is such a minor offense that it

IN THE OFFICE 2.2: Sitting With, Not Above

In the following counseling interaction I attempt to sit on a level plane with the client, identifying with her in her struggle. Still, I avoid condoning her sinful choices.

Marla: I got so drunk this week. And I hate that. It's not how I want to live. And I met this guy when I was drinking, and that was bad too.

Mark: You were trying to ease the pain, and this only made it worse. *[This is empathy mingled with agreement that her choices were unwise.]*

Marla: I feel so stupid when I do that. Like you say, it just makes everything worse. It costs money, I don't like the way I feel the next day, I wake up in someone else's apartment, and I have values about not sleeping around like that.

Mark: I see the struggle in you. You really want to turn a corner and make better choices. *[Though self-disclosure is not appropriate here, I identify with Marla's struggle because I experience the tug of sin in my life, too. My vulnerabilities are not the same as Marla's, but I encounter the same struggle between right and wrong—and sometimes I choose the wrong instead of right.]*

Marla: I want that so bad. This is not the life I want to be living. It's almost like I'm watching some other person make these choices that I would never make.

Of course it will also be important to help Marla make better choices in the future, but before discussing methods of accountability and behavior change it is important to empathize and understand her situation. This also helps build rapport and trust so that she will be more motivated when discussions of behavior change occur.

---

hardly deserves attention, and yet when we look around at a market economy we see that it is exactly this propensity for profit that makes a market economy heartless and cruel to the disadvantaged. For me, having a plumber not show up was a minor inconvenience, but the larger implications of living in a me-first, market-driven world is profoundly harming to billions of people around the globe. Still, we have come to rely on a certain amount of heartlessness and self-centered behavior. The eighteenth-century Scottish philosopher Adam Smith recognized that one person's self-interest could help control another's, and so the very reason that his free market system seems to work better than any other is that it acknowledges—even presumes—a certain level of sinfulness in human motivation. I called another plumber, spending my money and sending my future business elsewhere, because after all, it is my self-interest that will ultimately mitigate the self-interest of the plumber who failed to show up at the scheduled time. In this example, which is silly in its triviality, we see the complex mire of sin's consequences. Who is to say that the plumber is any more selfish for going to fix a wealthy person's toilet than I am for taking my business elsewhere? Both of us are functioning on principles of self-interest, and both of us are inflicting consequences on the other. The effects of sin reverberate through all creation. None of us is exempt.

Each of us has been sinned against—ranging from life-changing offenses, such as childhood sexual abuse, to relatively forgettable offenses, such as being cut off or flipped off on the expressway. These sins against us are harmful in various ways—sometimes physically, usually emotionally and always spiritually. They tear the relational fabric of God's creation, causing us to be increasingly isolated and cynical.

It is easier to see how others have hurt us than it is to see how we have hurt others. With each word of criticism and act of selfishness, we hurt those in our path. With every angry honk on the expressway, every vengeful attitude and action, and every word of gossip, we add to the sin problem. Sin is damaging, whether it is others' sin against us or our sin against others.

Counselors understand the consequences of sin because they so often work with clients deeply damaged by the offenses of others. The horrors of abuse, betrayal, abandonment, crime, racism and other injustices can never be dismissed with a casual comment about the ubiquity of sin: "Oh, we're just all a mess and the world is a broken place." No, these tragedies need to be named and grieved because just as God hates sin, so we ought to also. But we cannot have the same vantage point as God. God transcends the fallenness of our world and can hate sin from the perspective of utter righteousness (though God, revealed in Christ, chose to enter into the mess and live among us). In contrast, we are mired in the very problem we hate. We should still hate sin, but our complicity in the problems of this world also calls us to empathy and compassion, both for the precious people who are wounded by the sins of others and for those who commit the sins. They are, after all, the same people. They are us.

Forgiveness, Guilt and Shame

Several topics of mutual interest to theologians and psychologists help us understand this large view of sin and how it relates to a person's capacity for empathy. For example, the topic of forgiveness has gained enormous attention in mental health circles over the past twenty years (e.g., Worthington, 2005), and it has held longstanding interest to theologians (e.g., Jones, 1995; Shults & Sandage, 2003). One of the most important and intriguing ideas is the connection between forgiveness and empathy. Everett Worthington Jr., a leading expert in the psychology of forgiveness, articulates the "REACH" model for forgiving someone who has behaved wrongly (Worthington, 2003):

R   Recall the Hurt

E   Empathize

A   Altruistic Gift of Forgiveness

C   Commit Publicly to Forgive

H   Hold On to Forgiveness

Because recalling the hurt is a very natural thing to do—almost automatic for most people—experiencing empathy for the transgressor is the first arduous step in Worthington's model. Put another way, we might say that a posture of unforgiveness begins with an inability or unwillingness to empathize with an offender: "You are unlike me, more horrible and despicable than I could ever be." In contrast, an empathic attitude, with the potential of leading to forgiveness, might be, "You did something I have never done, and I am deeply hurt by it, but I've done some bad things too so I can begin to understand how this might have happened." Notice this is not merely empathy for an offender, it is empathy with the human condition. All of us are born in a sinful state, all are sinners by choice and habit, and all have been wounded by the sinfulness and sins of others.

Christians embed their understanding of forgiveness in an awareness of God's grace. God, who created us for relationship, has restored relationship with us through the forgiveness of our sins. And if we have been forgiven so much by a perfect God, then who are we to withhold forgiveness from our brothers or sisters who sin against us? (See, for example, Mt 6:14-15; 18:21-35.) This is a sort of theologically informed empathy that does not excuse or minimize sin—indeed, the cost of sin is devastating and reaches to every corner of creation—but recognizes that all of us are in the same deplorable state: in desperate need of God's redemption.

The difference between Augustine and Pelagius is not simply some abstract theological concept. It has practical, everyday implications for how we treat one another. Augustine's view lends itself to Worthington's REACH model by suggesting that we *all* fall short, we all harm others with our sinful dispositions and choices. There is no excuse for our sin—we remain morally culpable for the damage we do to others and to ourselves—but Augustine would have us recognize our own frailty in the misconduct of others. There is great tragedy embedded in the doctrine of original sin but also the possibility for compassionate empathy.

The topics of guilt and shame have also been studied by both psychologists and theologians. Guilt is an appropriate response to willful acts of sin and the consequences of those sins. Guilt can wake us up, cause us to grieve our wrongdoing, bring us empathic sorrow for those we have hurt and draw us to a place of confession and repentance. Because we have largely lost the language of sin in today's society, we sometimes treat guilt with disdain, as if it is neurotic baggage from a repressive time in human history. Sadly, some theories in psychology—especially those most prone to get media attention—sometimes undermine healthy guilt, assuming that good mental health means always thinking positive thoughts about oneself. This trite view of human experience is changing as recent findings in psychology have demonstrated that guilt can have positive implications. A sense of guilt over a specific misdeed is associated with empathy for the pain caused to others (Tangney, 1991; Tangney & Dearing, 2002). If I hurt you and feel a healthy sense of guilt, it will help me understand the pain you are in.

In contrast, shame is self-focused and unspecific. Guilt says, "I did something wrong, I hurt you deeply, and I feel terrible about it." Shame says, "I am a bad person and feel terrible about myself." Guilt helps us focus on the other; shame absorbs us in self-pity and self-recrimination. Guilt is an appropriate response to our acts of sin because, when we sin, we hurt others and we grieve God.

IN THE OFFICE 2.3: Promoting Guilt over Shame

Guilt promotes empathy by allowing one to see how personal choices have harmed others. Shame inhibits empathy by promoting self-focus. Notice, in the following example, how a therapist can help nudge a client away from shame and toward a more empathic other-oriented perspective.

Trina: I feel so terrible about the things I said to Susan yesterday. She was just stopping by my cubicle all day, and eventually I just told her how much she was bugging me. I called her a nuisance or something like that, and then last night I just felt terrible about it.

Mark: It's been weighing on your mind.
[This is a simple reflection to encourage her to keep talking about this incident and her feelings about it.]

Trina: Yeah. I mean, she's a friend of mine. And I shouldn't treat friends like that. Sometimes I think I am such a bad person, such a bad friend. I mean, who does that? Who talks to their friends like that?

Mark: You're pretty upset with yourself. I wonder what that was like for Susan.
[Note the effort to turn Trina's attention to Susan, helping her move toward other-oriented guilt rather than self-focused shame.]

Trina: I'm sure it was terrible. She likes me so much. I can just tell. And then when I treat her like that, she probably feels like someone has just trampled all over her.

Paradoxically, shame will make Trina more self-absorbed and therefore more vulnerable to hurt Susan in the future. Guilt helps Trina see things from Susan's perspective, and will help Trina act differently in the future.

Concluding Thoughts

The point of this synopsis of sin is not that we are as bad as we can be. Of course we are not. The Christian doctrine of total depravity does not mean that we are utterly vile in every conceivable way. Rather, it means that every dimension of human life has been contaminated—at least to some extent—by sin. We are all in need of grace.

The point is that we, as sinful humans, can never be good enough to earn God's kindness. Our sinfulness is bigger than we want to imagine. Only as we begin to grasp the immensity of the sin problem are we able to glimpse the depth of God's grace, and paradoxically, seeing God's grace gives us courage to face our sinfulness.

God is not merely a law-giver who expresses disappointment when we fall short. God is a lover who has relentlessly pursued humanity from the beginning of creation, seeking relationship at great cost. God is redeeming all creation, sanctifying and sustaining us today and calling us to hope in a glorious future.

Some people may avoid a language of sin because it makes them feel small and frail. Nothing could be further from the truth. The honest language of sin prepares us to see our infinite value in the arms of God, to breathe in the fragrance of life-giving love, and then to offer that love lavishly to ourselves and others. Spiritual leader Richard J. Foster reflects: "And so it is. If I know, really know, that God loves me, everything is changed. I am no longer a trifling speck in a meaningless cosmos. I am an eternal creature of infinite worth living in a universe animated by love and care and friendship" (1995, p. xiv).

3

The Healing Power of Grace

GREG WAS RELEASED FROM HIS PASTORATE when his adulterous affair became known, and he hobbled into my office for some help pulling his life back together. Predictably, he was defensive at first, minimizing what he had done and the pain he had caused his family and congregation. Rather than confront his self-deception, I listened and cared for this broken man. Greg had not experienced much grace in his life, so he could not afford to speak a language of sin. Paradoxically, he had preached many sermons about sin and grace, but these were theological concepts, ideas from books read in seminary rather than transforming life experiences. Raised in a family where he could never quite please his demanding parents, Greg married a good woman, Kathy, who had difficulty affirming him, and he entered a profession where perfection is the only tolerable standard. Greg had spent a lifetime running from his sin, never admitting his weakness because there were no arms of grace to catch him if he fell. My job was to catch him. As he began to feel safe—after several weeks of meeting together—his tears began to flow. His sin came into focus. Greg began to see the horrible truth of how he had betrayed Kathy, his children and his congregation. He shed tears of sorrow over his sin. He grieved his childhood, how he had longed for someone to express tender care for him regardless of his grades or athletic prowess. Greg spoke words of repentance and begged loved ones for forgiveness. This time his words were not from theology books but from his heart. He spoke and wept the language of sin, but only after he had a glimpse of grace.

Though chapters in a book must come in a particular order, and I have chosen to write a chapter about sin before a chapter about grace, it is important to keep in mind that a Christian understanding of sin and grace does not lend itself to linearity. It's not that we sin first and then need grace. Grace is a pervasive part of God's character and purposes and has been from all eternity. The gracious character of God was evident in Eden before sin corrupted a good creation, as it will be evident in the new heaven and earth that Christians anticipate. God's grace is evident in the *imago Dei,* some of which survived the Fall and characterizes our relationships with one another. Grace is not something to withhold until after a person admits sin; Greg was able to see his sin because he experienced a measure of grace in our counseling.

In chapter two I suggested that counseling is a place of empathy and that empathy can be enhanced by a sound doctrine of sin. In addition to empathy, counseling is also a place of discovery and recovery, both of which are enhanced by an understanding of grace.

Discovery and Recovery

In counseling, we help clients *dis*cover previously unexplored areas of their lives. As the word implies, this involves peeling back the defensive cover of life and exploring the parts of life that are rarely considered or discussed. Every major counseling theory—psychodynamic, humanistic, cognitive behavioral, family systems and biblical—involves investigating the unexplored areas of life.

When I go to the physician for a physical, I am taken aback by how quickly the nurse hands me a paper robe, tells me to disrobe and says the doctor will be in soon. Disrobing is not such an innocuous thing, so I always find it a shocking reality that my doctor only sees me that way. I sometimes wonder if he would even recognize me if we ran into each other at the hardware store or in church; after all, he has never seen me in clothes! But however shocking I find disrobing for my annual physical, we ask much more of our counseling clients. We ask them to become psychologically naked, revealing their unexplored motives and feelings and conflicts. It is a far more difficult thing to describe a childhood history of abuse, a current addiction, a spiritual crisis or a relationship that is falling apart than to take one's clothes off and slip on a paper robe.

Each year at my physical I wish someone would turn up the thermostat a couple degrees. It is difficult enough to sit in that paper robe, but it is worse yet while shivering in a cold office. When Greg came to my office after his church released him, my first task was to adjust the thermostat so that he was comfortable. I do not mean this literally, of course; the office temperature was fine. But I needed to create a safe environment where he could feel as comfortable as possible before he would be willing to consider his need to become psychologically naked in my presence. Greg needed a

COUNSELING TIP 3.1: *Defenses and Noetic Effects*

One of the enduring influences of Sigmund Freud and his daughter, Anna Freud, is their notion of defense mechanisms. Though some of Freud's ideas are vigorously challenged by Christians, defense mechanisms ought to be considered. Defenses shield us from the harsh edge of truth. For example, if I am a jealous and controlling person, it may be easier to see my friends as jealous and controlling—projecting my problems onto them—rather than honestly acknowledging my problem. Or if I have a traumatic memory from childhood, I might choose not to think about it (suppression) in order to avoid the emotional pain it causes. Defense mechanisms also make sense from a Christian perspective. Theologians speak of the noetic effects of sin, meaning that our sin blinds us in various ways from an honest look at ourselves and our need for God. It is difficult to see our problem with pride, for example, because of our pride.

It is almost never helpful to attack defenses head on. If a counselor pronounces, "You have a pride problem," or "You are denying how greedy you are," it is likely to evoke even more defensiveness in the client. Counselors who use such tactics may actually make their clients worse by "thickening" their defensive style. When a client becomes defensive, it is usually better to offer an observation than a confrontation. For example, "I notice how upsetting it is for you when your wife disagrees with you." Helping a client understand defenses is a gradual process of discovery that occurs in the context of a safe, confiding counseling relationship. Counselors should not force or hurry the process.

context of grace before he could venture into a fuller awareness of his sin. Grace is an essential aspect—a prerequisite—of *dis*covery in counseling.

Counseling also involves *re*covery. After the defensive layers are peeled back and the nakedness of the psychological and spiritual struggle is revealed, a client needs to rebuild a life that has hope and faith and love. This is also a process of grace because recovery occurs best in the context of a safe, confiding relationship. Every time Kathy exploded in anger toward Greg—which seemed quite understandable given the circumstances—he would hobble back into my office broken by shame. Each time I needed to contain his sadness with kindness and merciful understanding. I needed to create a safe place so that he could see once again how deeply he had hurt his lifelong partner. This happened time after time in our work together until he slowly began to recover his identity as a broken and sinful man who is deeply loved by God. Greg and Kathy also sought help from a marital therapist where they were able to recover their marriage.

To some extent discovery and recovery in counseling do not require either the counselor or the client to be a Christian. Therapists of all persuasions craft safe, grace-filled relationships with their clients as they discuss previously-unexplored conflicts, suppressed and repressed feelings, difficult relationships, and so on. This safe therapeutic relationship is one of the major reasons why clients recover, leaving therapy feeling and functioning better than when they started. But then again, some measure of recovery may not be possible apart from awareness of God's grace revealed in Jesus Christ. Only when we understand how profoundly God loves and pursues us are we able to rest in a deep, abiding sense of peace and acceptance.

Christians believe that this human form of grace—which exists in relationships among people who may not acknowledge God at all—is made possible because of God's grace to humanity. Many theologians since the Reformation have distinguished between the *common grace* available to all people and the *special grace* that draws people to abundant life in Christ. All the various blessings of life, including the capacity to be gracious with one another, are made possible because of God's common grace, though it often functions beneath the threshold of human awareness. Common grace is available in every counseling relationship regardless of the religious val-

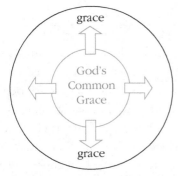
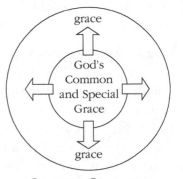

MOST COUNSELING PARADIGMS
Common grace is at work, but often beneath the awareness of counselor.

CHRISTIAN COUNSELING
Both common and special grace are at work and may be discussed.

Figure 3.1. Perspectives on discovery and recovery

ues of the participants (see figure 3.1). In Christian counseling, grace is a more explicit part of the counseling process and special grace functions alongside common grace. Special grace is both justifying (*dis*covering our state and setting us right with God) and sanctifying (*re*covering, helping us to grow in our Christian life). Notice that both common and special grace are restorative, helping to draw people back into right relationships. This reveals something important about God's character and purposes.

Common Grace

The word *grace* is slippery. It means many different things in different contexts. In the thirteenth-century *Summa Theologica,* Thomas Aquinas described three meanings: being held in someone's favor, a gift that is freely given or a response to a gift freely given. These are, of course, highly related. If person A gives a gift to person B, it is because person A holds person B in a position of favor, and it is likely that person B will respond gratefully to the gift that is given. In the New Testament, we see these same meanings: grace (*cháris* in the original language) as an attitude of favor (e.g., Lk 2:52), as a gift freely given (e.g., 1 Cor 16:3) and as a response of gratitude to that gift (e.g., Rom 6:17). But the New Testament reveals even more diversity with *cháris*. The same Greek root is also used to describe kind and lovely speech (e.g., Lk 4:22), a spiritual gift to serve the church (e.g., Rom 12:3) and future heavenly blessings (e.g., 1 Pet 1:13). And our contemporary English has introduced more diversity yet; grace is used to describe delicate movements of the human body (e.g., "the ballerina has such grace"), kindness (e.g., "you are a gracious host"), leniency (e.g., "I will grant you some grace on when the assignment is due") and so on.

In this broad and diverse sense, grace can be seen in all aspects of counseling. Counselors come to feel favor for their clients, and vice versa. A counselor "graces" a client with favor, kindness, attention and compassion. The client feels grateful for these things, and may offer words of grace to the counselor. A counselor may be lenient at times, choosing not to charge a client for a missed session, for example. Even physical movements of the counselor, such as leaning forward in one's chair during intense moments of emotional pain, can be graceful.

After many years of providing Christian counseling and studying the scientific literature on psychotherapy, I am convinced that counseling works in large part because it is a place of common grace. Psychotherapists speak of relationship factors, which are things that all counseling approaches share in common, such as empathy, a confiding relationship, a safe environment, trust, discussing feelings and so on (Lambert, 2004). Though psychotherapy researchers tend not to use the word *grace,* almost all of the common factors are enhanced when a therapist acts graciously toward the client. Relationship factors are approximately twice as important as counseling techniques in determining how a person responds (Lambert, 1992). Effective counselors provide a safe place where acceptance and kindness abound, a place where struggle and brokenness can be openly explored and grieved without the fear of judgment. This frees people to look honestly at themselves, to become more open in their other relationships, and to move forward into richer and deeper connections with those they love.

This sort of grace brings people out of hiding into places of discovery and recovery. As a new counselor just out of graduate school, I thought my task was to help people with their depression, anxiety, relationship problem or whatever else they described as troublesome. But the longer I have done this work, the more aware I have become that many psychological problems have a common essence—a deeper existential restlessness—that resides beneath whatever symptoms may be targeted in our list of treatment goals. Depression is not only about sadness, for example. Within the first few months of counseling it is likely that depressed clients will feel safe enough to begin exploring and expressing anger. If talking about anger feels safe, sometime later these same clients may begin to explore their haunting fears and their deep sense of loneliness and isolation. Counseling becomes a process of bringing hidden feelings and conflicts out in the open where they can be better understood and reevaluated, but this will only happen if the counselor is a safe, gracious presence in the client's life.

One counselor may squash the first explorations of anger by pronouncing that anger is sinful and not tolerated in counseling, in which case the client will simply go back into hiding. Another therapist will listen nonjudgmentally, serving as a safe companion for the client's explorations. The kind, attentive therapist who is willing to sit with messy emotions gives a client confidence to keep discovering conflicts, beliefs and relational patterns that have done damage in their undiscovered state. Discussions of anger often uncover fear, and discussions of fear often uncover loneliness.

Coincidentally, the therapist who squashes anger, calling it sinful, may be doctrinally correct. Scripture and early Christian literature are replete with instructions to control our anger (Prov 14:29; 15:1; Jas 1:19-20); anger is often described as a dangerous and damaging moral quality (Prov 15:18; Mt 5: 21-22; Gal 5:19-20; see also Okholm, 2001). It is contemporary religious myth—fostered mostly by Christian counselors and psychologists—that anger is morally neutral. This is not to say that anger is always wrong, but we must be careful not to justify anger without considering the nuances of human brokenness. We are told in various Christian self-help books that Jesus was angry, so we should also feel fine about being angry. Such reasoning is quite flawed because Jesus was sinless, and we are not. Our human anger is almost always tinged with self-interest and neurotic ambition. These same self-help books cite Ephesians 4:26 over and over—as if daytime anger is sanctified but nocturnal anger immoral—while Ephesians 4:27 and 31 are conveniently ignored.

We seem to be left with three options regarding anger in Christian counseling writings, with the first two being more common than the third:

OPTION 1: Anger is morally neutral or perhaps even good (after all, Jesus got angry, and the Bible says to be angry but not to sin), therefore our goal in counseling is to help people explore and understand their anger.

OPTION 2: Anger is tainted with sin (after all, the majority of references to anger in Scripture and virtually all early Christian writers on the topic assume that anger is morally suspect), therefore our primary goal in counseling is to help bring people to conviction and repentance regarding their anger. This is often done through direct words of confrontation.

Option 1 seems to be the prevalent position among Christian counselors, but it requires hermeneutic distortion when approaching Scripture. Option 2 is theologically better, but it will drive counseling clients further into hiding. Option 3 is a grace-filled option, one that recognizes conviction of sin often comes indirectly through an effective counseling relationship rather than directly through confrontational words by the counselor.

OPTION 3: Human anger is tainted with sin, but it is still worth exploring because the greatest sources of evil in our lives are the forces and passions we have not yet *dis*covered. This sort of approach to Christian counseling acknowledges both sin and grace, with the goal of moving people forward toward greater understanding of self, others and God. Anger ought to be explored in counseling without a counselor being critical or condemning. Sometimes clients will experience conviction for their anger, but that conviction will come from a place of interpersonal safety, self-awareness and the work of the Holy Spirit, and only rarely from a counselor's words of confrontation.

IN THE OFFICE 3.1: Option 3: Exploring Anger Without Condoning It

How can a Christian counselor help a client explore feelings of anger without implying that anger is good? It is possible to do both by combining gentle confrontation with a compassionate desire to help the client discover unresolved feelings and conflicts.

Henry: I have been so ticked off at my Dad for so many years about this. You know, parents are supposed to love their children. But some woman comes along, he falls in love and what happened to him loving us? All he cared about was himself. He thought it would make him happy, and he sacrificed us to make it happen.

Mark: It must have felt terrible.

Henry: Yeah, and it still does. I will never be able to forgive him for what he did.

Mark: The anger has a grip on you.

Henry: What? Do you think I shouldn't be angry?

Mark: I think the anger is very reasonable. But it has its teeth in you, doesn't it?

Henry: Yeah, I suppose. But wouldn't you be angry too? I mean, if your father left his family just because he got turned on by some other woman.

Mark: I'm sure anyone would feel angry. It was a selfish thing, a devastating thing to do.

Henry: He never contacted me after he left. I mean maybe a few times on my birthday or Christmas, but he never took any effort to know me.

Mark: That has left some deep scars.

Henry: It hurt more than anything in my life. It still does.

Mark: Maybe the anger helps protect you from that hurt.

Henry: I suppose. It's easier to feel angry at him than to wonder why he didn't want anything to do with me.

Rather than condoning the anger, or spending time debating its moral valence, it seems better to look beneath the anger and find the deeper sources of pain and struggle.

If fear and shame drive people into hiding, grace brings them out. As Adam and Eve hid their nakedness behind fig leaves, so we hide our sense of shame behind denial and distortion. Yet something is woven into the human soul that makes us vaguely unhappy about hiding. Deep down we want to search the inward places, to acknowledge our pain and struggles, to seek reconciliation. It is grace that bids us to come out of hiding.

The interpersonal grace that calls people out of hiding is quite spectacular, even if we call its source common grace (it is only "common" insofar as it is available to all). God is the author of all grace and goodness wherever it is found in creation, and all humanity is blessed by God's beneficence. But for the Christian there is another sort of grace, a stunning and miraculous special grace that changes everything.

Special Grace

The Bible speaks of a powerful, life-changing grace whereby God grants eternal favor to those who could never deserve such a thing. This special grace is principally evident in the apostle Paul's writings:

> For everyone has sinned; we all fall short of God's glorious standard. Yet God, with his undeserved kindness, declares that we are righteous. He did this through Christ Jesus when he freed us from the penalty of our sins. (Rom 3:23-24)

> I do not treat the grace of God as meaningless. For if keeping the law could make us right with God, then there was no need for Christ to die. (Gal 2:21)

> But God is so rich in mercy, and he loved us so much, that even though we were dead because of our sins, he gave us life when he raised Christ from the dead. (It is only by God's grace that you have been saved!) For he raised us from the dead along with Christ and seated us with him in the heavenly realms because we united with Christ Jesus. So God can point to us in all future ages as examples of the incredible wealth of his grace and kindness toward us, as shown in all he has done for us who are united with Christ Jesus. (Eph 2:4-7)

> For God saved us and called us to live a holy life. He did this, not because we deserved it, but because that was his plan from before the beginning of time— to show us his grace through Christ Jesus. (2 Tim 1:9)

Special grace is bestowed by God on undeserving individuals, leading them to an abundant life in Christ both now and through eternity. Special grace justifies us before God and sanctifies us as we grow in wisdom and character.

Walter Elwell, a biblical scholar and former colleague at Wheaton College, taught me a helpful distinction between kindness, mercy and grace. A kind person is caring and gentle. Mercy is a particular sort of kindness; mercy is kindness to those who *do not* deserve it. Grace is a subset of mercy; grace is merciful kindness to those who *cannot* deserve it. We often see kindness in daily interactions. I compliment my wife for the cheerful, loving way she wakes each morning, and she tells me later that evening how she appreciates the way I interact with our children. Perhaps she gives me a back rub before we fall off to sleep in the evening, and I give her a back rub in the morning. In these examples we make positive exchanges, following the social contract implicit in all satisfying relationships (I'll be nice to you, and you be nice to me), and at least according to social exchange theory our relationship is likely to do quite well under these circumstances. This is a relationship based on mutual kindness. But what if I am particularly grumpy some day, criticizing Lisa for the way she drives and parents and brushes her teeth, and in response she looks at me and says how glad she is that she married me? This is more than kindness, more than I deserve. This is mercy: kindness expressed to one who does not deserve it. Now fastforward twenty-five years into the future. I now have advanced Alzheimer's disease and struggle with the most basic functions. My personality has changed so that I am suspicious, accusing and angry. Without constant attention I would be dangerous to myself or others, and I would surely end up lost and alone. My wife continues to show kindness, though she receives little appreciation. Not only do I not deserve her kindness, but I can never again function in a way that makes me worthy of a kind social exchange. She is extending grace: merciful kindness to one who cannot deserve it.

If we view God apart from our sin, we may see God's kindness. We may call it grace, but that is some combination of semantic confusion and sloppy doctrine. Only when we apprehend the depth of our transgression, the ubiquity of our sin problem, our inability to escape sin, and God's abhorrence of sin can we really grasp the meaning of grace. Grace is merciful kindness offered by God to those who *do not* and *cannot ever* deserve God's kindness, and it is our only hope.

The debate between Pelagius and Augustine, described briefly in chapter two, is significant for understanding the nature of God in relationship to humankind. Ultimately the church sided with Augustine, and the doctrine of grace became something that John Newton rightly described as *amazing* many centuries later. The apostle Paul put it this way: "Now, most people would not be willing to die for an upright person, though someone might perhaps be willing to die for a person who is especially good. But God showed his great love for us by sending Christ to die for us while we were still sinners" (Rom 5:7-8). We are bent souls living in a fallen world; we cannot deserve God's favor, but in grace God extends kindness nonetheless. Grace resides in God's character and has nothing to do with our capacity to deserve it.

The Christian doctrine of sin can seem like a dismal proposition unless it is coupled with the doctrine of grace. Taken together, a Christian view of sin and grace brings enormous hope. We do not have to perform at a certain level to obtain God's favor. God's favor is a given; it comes first. We have nothing to earn from God, nothing to prove. Then, in grace, God continues to help us grow in faithfulness and holiness.

Four Concepts Pertaining to Grace

Grace is not easy to grasp. It runs counter to so many of the cultural messages surrounding us. J. I. Packer (1973) describes four concepts people misunderstand, all of which limit our understanding of grace: moral depravity, God's retributive justice, our spiritual impotence and the sovereignty of God. Though Packer's intent was not to discuss counseling, it is fascinating to see how these same four concepts affect the work of Christian counselors.

Moral depravity. A Christian view of grace presumes that humans are fallen and morally culpable before God. Those who do not accept this premise—those who believe they are fundamentally good and worthy of God's love, if there is a God—cannot fully understand the Christian doctrine of grace.

A fundamental premise of contemporary life seems to be, "I'm okay." But if we are all okay, then why do we live in a bloody, violent world? Why is the ten o'clock news so depressingly replete with murders, scandals, abuse and corruption? Even when we misbehave, rather than challenging the assumption of our moral goodness, we tend to explain it as the result of bad reinforcement patterns or depleted neurotransmitters or poor parenting or a lack of adequate self-esteem or stifled drives for autonomy. All these explanations may be correct in a way, but they fail to account for the full weight of the human moral problem. All our shortcomings—including those related to neurotransmitters and bad parenting—reflect the sinful condition of our world, to which we contribute. If we fail to see the magnitude of our sin problem, then grace devolves into a notion of a God who is merely lenient and understanding. Such a view of God's grace is much too small, because our view of sin is too small.

In his provocative book *Blue Like Jazz*, Donald Miller describes how he wants to go to a political protest someday and hold up a placard that reads, "I am the problem." Donald Miller is right. He is the problem. And so am I. You are too. The moral depravity of several billion human beings adds up to a world that cannot begin to fit all the bad events of the day into the ten o'clock news.

> I think every conscious person, every person who is awake to the functioning principles within his reality, has a moment where he stops blaming the problems in the world on group think, on humanity and authority, and starts to face himself. I hate this more than anything. This is the hardest principle within Christian spirituality for me to deal with. The problem is not out there; the problem is the needy beast of a thing that lives in my chest. (Miller, 2003, p. 20)

It is also true, of course, that there is good news. We see tremendous beauty and goodness in the world and in every human being, but it resides side-by-side with moral depravity. No aspect of creation is unstained by sin.

A few counselors I have known over the years seem to function as self-esteem brokers, but if Christianity is true then it means they are overlooking something more authentic, and ultimately much better, than self-esteem. When we treat love as something we are entitled to, as if any reasonable human or deity would be silly not to love us, we overlook the possibility that God's grace is more powerful, important, and healing than positive self-talk and self-esteem will ever be.

I recall sitting in a small group with a young woman who had recently had a spiritual awakening. She described her childhood in a home where self-esteem was the primary virtue. Her parents taught her that she was delightful, talented, good-hearted, intelligent and witty. Having spent several months in a small group with her, I tended to agree with her parents—she was the kind of young woman that anyone would love to have as a daughter. But as she talked about her spiritual awakening, she acknowledged that something important was missing from her incubator of childhood self-esteem. Somehow, deep down, she always knew that she was not quite as great as her parents thought she was. She knew there was an intrinsic need

---

IN THE OFFICE 3.2: I Am the Problem

Donald Miller's idea of carrying a political placard that reads "I am the problem" reminds me of a common situation in the counseling office. It is always easier to see the problem in another person than it is in ourselves. Sometimes counselors can use gentle probes, words of confrontation, and strategic silence to help clients see their personal contribution to a problem.

Neil: I don't understand why she wanted children. We were happy before. Now we just deal with snot and crying and chaos. Our marriage is struggling, we can't sleep at night, and it's all since having children.

Mark: These feelings seem particularly intense for you today.

Neil: Yeah, I didn't get much sleep. Caleb and Samantha were both up during the night. Caleb ended up in our bed, and I can never sleep with him thrashing all around. I'm really struggling with all this.

Mark: Yes, I imagine being fatigued adds to your sense of loss. At times like this it feels like you've lost your marriage.

Neil: It really does. And then I get angry at Jessica. I suppose I really need to figure out how to forgive her for this.

Mark: Forgive her?

Neil: Yeah, you know, for wanting children.

Mark: It might be worth thinking about. I'm just wondering, though, because the word *forgive* implies that Jessica wanting children is wrong and needs to be forgiven.

Neil: Well, I didn't want children and she did.

[silence]

Neil: I guess I see what you mean. Maybe wanting children is just as legitimate as not wanting them.

---

for healing, an inner darkness, a moral decay, which was also part of her character. As she ventured into the teenage traps of promiscuity and drugs, she felt like an imposter, as if no one could know about her true self or else they would stop loving her. She didn't need another self-esteem button or

sticker to wear around the house. What she longed for was authentic awareness of her good and bad qualities, and love that was big enough to embrace her regardless of her sin. When she turned to God as a young adult,
she found what she had been longing for—One who knew every dark corner of her soul and still loved her—relentlessly and eternally. In God, whose
character is revealed in Jesus (Col 1:15; Heb 1:3), she found forgiveness, acceptance and grace. Self-esteem and positive self-talk could not meet her
deepest need. A sound theology of sin and grace was her only hope.

God's retributive justice. Today's world is filled with choices. Lisa and
I frequent a restaurant that has a make-your-own-pasta menu. By marking
a few ovals on a scanner-friendly menu, the customer has complete control
over the meal that is served a few minutes later. I can choose whole wheat
penne pasta with marinara sauce, spinach, olives and artichoke hearts. Or I
could choose any of several million other permutations, depending on my
culinary whims. Best of all, I can avoid unseemly additions to pasta such as
anchovies.

I have noticed that many contemporary Christians tend to approach their
faith in the same menu-oriented fashion. We select the doctrines we like and
find agreeable, and choose not to select other doctrines that we find distaste-
ful. We check the box for a loving God who dances over us in joy, but
choose not to believe in a God who punishes sin. But, "God is not true to
himself unless he punishes sin. And unless one knows and feels the truth of
this fact, that wrongdoers have no natural hope of anything from God but
retributive judgment, one can never share the biblical faith in divine grace"
(Packer, 1973, p. 131).

In many Christian circles, grace has been separated from the retributive
consequences of sin, and thereby it is reduced to kindness, compassion or
understanding. These are virtuous qualities that should be affirmed and cel-
ebrated, but none of them come close to the importance of the Christian notion of grace. In Christianity we can only understand grace when we understand the cost of sin. When we leave sin out of the story, as we often try to
do, our historic theological vocabulary is supplanted by a shallow popularized psychology and theology. We end up with what German theologian
Dietrich Bonhoeffer described as cheap grace. Bonhoeffer distinguished between cheap grace and costly grace: "Cheap grace is the deadly enemy of
our Church. . . . In such a Church the world finds a cheap covering for its
sins; no contrition is required, still less any real desire to be delivered from

sin. Cheap grace therefore amounts to a denial of the living Word of God, in fact, a denial of the Incarnation of the Word of God" (Bonhoeffer, 1959, pp. 45-46). In contrast, costly grace recognizes the amazing character of a God who has relentlessly pursued fallen humanity.

In love and righteousness God established an order of living that would promote harmony and peace. This order of living reflects God's righteous and holy character and God's desire for relationship with humanity. God abides by this order of living and administers the same standards of justice to all humanity. If we could live by God's order, then our lives would be filled with intimate relationships and shalom, but in our sinful condition we cannot and do not live the way God desires. The cost of sin is great to all humanity—separation from the divine. We are east of Eden, wandering in a world that has drifted far from God's loving order. We see the price of sin as nations and families wage war, the strong oppress the weak, and unimaginable hedonism is touted as human freedom. Sin is a "vicious and mortal enemy, an irascible and persistent power" (Berkouwer, 1971, p. 235).

Today's experience of pain and suffering are just a small part of the story. Yes, we struggle and groan under the weight of sin (Rom 8:20-23), but the eternal consequences of sin—utter and permanent separation from God's loving and righteous character—are infinitely worse than what we now experience.

Many people stagnate at this point—trying to figure out how all this human suffering can occur when God is all-powerful and all-good, or how a loving God can damn people to eternal misery, or why the distribution of human suffering seems so haphazard and unequally distributed. These are fine questions worthy of exploration, but all of them keep us focused on the human cost of God's justice.

The story of the gospel goes well beyond the cost that humanity bears for sin. Because God's character is loving, the eternal "Word became flesh and made his dwelling among us" (Jn 1:14 TNIV). The magnificent humility and love of God is revealed in Christ. God is not sitting in a heavenly easy chair pushing pain and suffering buttons to inflict discomfort on humans at random moments in life; no, God is fiercely loving, working within the order that flows from God's righteous character to redeem fallen humanity.

> For God in all his fullness
>   was pleased to live in Christ,
> and through him God reconciled
>   everything to himself.

> He made peace with everything in heaven and on earth
>> by means of Christ's blood on the cross.
>
> This includes you who were once far away from God. You were his enemies,
> separated from him by your evil thoughts and actions. Yet now he has recon-
> ciled you to himself through the death of Christ in his physical body. As a re-
> sult, he has brought you into his own presence, and you are holy and
> blameless as you stand before him without a single fault. (Col 1:19-22)

The life and work of Christ is where God's justice and grace meet.

Counseling is not a place to promote cheap grace by implying that God
really doesn't care very much about the bad things we do. God does care.
Sin should not be minimized or glossed over with a menu-based, choose-
the-feature-that-you-want theology. Sin needs to be *dis*covered in the context of a safe and grace-filled relationship, tears of grief and repentance
shed, and the depth of God's forgiving grace encountered.

Spiritual impotence. Throughout history humans have attempted to ap-
pease God, or the gods. People have tried dancing in certain ways, sacrific-
ing the right animals (or even children!), mutilating their own bodies or others', restricting diets, praying with certain rituals, and so on. We will do
almost anything to resist the conclusion that we are helpless when it comes
to earning God's favor. Though the Pelagian controversy officially ended
with the Council of Carthage in A.D. 418, it has continued to plague the
church through all the centuries since. *Posse non peccare* (it is possible not
to sin) implied that we could somehow muster enough willpower to live a
life that is fully pleasing to God, but in asserting our power to satisfy God
we end up missing a far more hopeful possibility—that we are impotent in
our efforts to live up to God's design, and that our hope of redemption lies
in God's character rather than our personal efforts. "He saved us, not because of the righteous things we had done, but because of his mercy. He
washed away our sins, giving us a new birth and new life through the Holy
Spirit" (Tit 3:5). If this is true, then the title of Larry Crabb's (2002) book is
right—*The Pressure's Off: There's a New Way to Live*. Think about it. This
means we get off the treadmill and rest in the presence of the Almighty. Human effort is still important, but not in order to earn God's love. God's love
comes first, and then we are called and empowered toward holiness
through the process of sanctification.

In God's grace, justification comes first and sanctification follows. Most of
us would handle things the other way around: "Get your act together and

then you will find me much more forgiving and understanding." However backward it may seem in our human economy, God offers justifying grace first and then beckons us toward greater spiritual maturity. The words of Christ, offered to a woman caught in adultery, echo through the generations to all who have experienced the grace of God: "Neither do I [condemn you]. Go and sin no more" (Jn 8:11).

This has important implications for Christian counseling, because grace ought to come first in the counseling office also. Confrontation has its place, but only after the safety of grace has been established.

In Victor Hugo's masterpiece *Les Misérables,* Jean Valjean is a hardened and cynical ex-convict looking for a place to spend the night. Scorned by all the inns in town, he ends up at Monseigneur Bienvenu's house. Rather than sending Valjean away, the bishop welcomes the foul-smelling man into his home and provides a meal, which Valjean scarfs down like an animal. Then the priest offers him a place to sleep.

After everyone is asleep, Jean Valjean sneaks back into the kitchen, steals six silver plates and escapes into the night. Soldiers see him running, apprehend him, find the silver and bring him back to the bishop the following morning. But the bishop, rather than accuse the man and send him back to prison, goes to the mantle, collects two silver candlesticks, and hands them to Valjean, saying: "I gave you the candlesticks also, which are silver like the rest, and would bring two hundred francs. Why did you not take them along with the plates?" As the soldiers release Valjean and withdraw, Monseigneur Bienvenu draws close and speaks life-changing words of grace: "Jean Valjean, my brother: you belong no longer to evil, but to good. It is your soul that I am buying for you. I withdraw it from dark thoughts and from the spirit of perdition, and I give it to God!"

The apostle Paul instructs, "Therefore, accept each other just as Christ has accepted you, so that God will be given glory" (Rom 15:7). And when we do, as portrayed by Monseigneur Bienvenu, we free people to confront their spiritual impotence and need for God. Later that night, after stumbling through the day in a stupor, Valjean's eyes open to his sin.

> At the very moment when he exclaimed: "What a wretch I am!" he saw himself as he was, and was already so far separated from himself that it seemed to him that he was only a phantom, and that he had there before him, in flesh and bone with his stick in his hand, his blouse on his back, his knapsack filled with stolen articles on his shoulders, with his stern and gloomy face, and his

thoughts full of abominable projects, the hideous galley slave, Jean Valjean. . . .

He beheld himself then, so to speak, face to face. . . . Jean Valjean wept long. He shed hot tears, he wept bitterly. . . . He beheld his life, and it seemed to him horrible; his soul, and it seemed to him frightful. There was, however, a softened light upon that life and upon that soul. It seemed to him that he was looking upon Satan by the light of Paradise. (Hugo, 1997, pp. 80-119)

In the presence of grace we can afford to open our eyes to our sin.

Christian counseling involves grace that takes the pressure off. God does for us what we cannot do for ourselves. This sort of grace frees a person to move naturally toward honest discovery—about current life situations, conflicts and wounds from early life experiences, destructive patterns in relationships, dysfunctional beliefs, intrusive thoughts, persistent feelings and inner conflicts.

God's sovereignty. When I read spiritual classics, written long before the Enlightenment brought such enormous confidence in human reason, I am struck by the reverence people express toward God. Today it seems that we often get it backwards, as if we are the arbiters to decide whether God is doing a good job or a bad job. We exchange God's sovereignty for a sense

---

COUNSELING TIP 3.2: *Grace and Boundaries*

The example of Monseigneur Bienvenu in *Les Misérables* is a powerful illustration of how grace comes first; most people need to feel safe before they are able to take an honest look at their sin. But it is not a good metaphor of counseling, because effective counseling also involves setting clear expectations and boundaries in order to set a consistent therapeutic frame. Monseigneur Bienvenu had only one encounter with Jean Valjean, so he could show extravagant mercy without it changing their future relationship. If a counselor were to do something similar—give a financially strapped client $1000, for example, it would create unhealthy dependencies and change the nature of the helping relationship. Counselors do not show mercy by giving away silver candlesticks but by demonstrating kindness and consistency in a well-defined relationship. The most healing and grace-filled counseling encounters are characterized by an ongoing, caring relationship that becomes safe and predictable for the client.

of personal sovereignty. The Hollywood movie *Bruce Almighty* shows an angry man (Bruce) who questions God's goodness. So God lets Bruce be God for a while, and Bruce discovers it is not so easy to manage the universe. It is a whimsical premise that would have been unimaginable in another era. But today it seems we are quite intrigued with the idea of scrutinizing God according to our idiosyncratic notions of what is good and bad. People rushed to the movie, perhaps, because all of us wonder what it would be like to be Bruce Almighty or Evan Almighty or Susan Almighty or Mark Almighty or whomever Almighty.

Grace is a divine quality offered by a God who is free to grant grace or not. It is God's prerogative to offer unmerited kindness to sinful humanity. Divine grace presumes that one person, living above the mire of another, chooses to reach down in loving kindness and help an undeserving soul out of a deadly situation. This is what God offers—justifying grace to save us from the dismal consequences of our sin, and sanctifying grace to keep us from diving back into the mire the first chance we get. Discussions of God's sovereignty typically stir up debates about predestination and free will. These are important theological discussions that fall outside the realm of this book. Still, it is important to recognize that God is God and we are not. God has the choice to offer grace or not, and God makes the first move whether it is a prevenient grace extended to all people (as the Wesleyans suggest) or an irresistible grace offered to the elect (as Calvinists suggest).

Christian counselors speak and write a good deal about expressing feelings toward God these days, whatever our feelings may be. This need not be alarming in itself—indeed, we see Israel's King David, the "man after God's own heart," express anger and disappointment and confusion toward God throughout the Psalms. Counseling needs to be a place of authentic discovery, even if the negative feelings are directed toward the divine. But we need to be cautious because open anger at God can easily devolve into a narcissistic style of questioning God's sovereignty. Anger need not undermine God's sovereignty; David expressed his feelings in the context of acknowledging that God is faithful and good, even in the most confusing moments of life. David found balance between open expression of his feelings and affirming God's sovereignty.

Perhaps the ultimate expression of a self-focused view of God is seen among counselors who teach clients to "forgive God." Interpersonal forgiveness is a good thing, a time-honored and godly virtue, but the notion of for-giving God is wrong-headed because it presumes that God has done some-thing wrong that needs to be forgiven. If God is capable of doing wrong, then it presumes that some human standard has been established by which God should be evaluated. The creature is evaluating the goodness of the Creator—a dismaying and appalling reversal of sovereignty.

A friend of mine went through a tragic year involving the sudden death of a family member, recovery from heart bypass surgery, challenges with his grown children, financial difficulty, job loss and many other things. It was an awful year, and he struggled the entire time with frustration, disappoint-ment and anger. But I still recall what he said in the middle of that terrible year: "My theme for the year is that God is good all of the time." Even in the face of tragedy, and while he was being open about the painful emotions he experienced, he still affirmed the sovereignty and goodness of God. Faith means we affirm God's goodness even when God seems far away, even in the midst of doubts, disappointments, anger and grief.

Counselors are wise to help clients discover feelings of anger, bitterness and resentment, even if those feelings are directed toward God. This is part of the discovery process, and it is facilitated by a gracious counselor who listens well without being overly alarmed or judgmental. But God is still sov-ereign and good beyond measure. God's grace is greater than all our sins, all our good works, and all our doubts and questions.

In chapter two, I argued that the doctrine of sin ought to be a basis of empathy in Christian counseling because every Christian understands what it is to have a problem with sin. And this is precisely why God's sovereign perspective is impossible for the Christian counselor to attain: we cannot stand outside our sin problem to rescue another person. To suggest we can is to cheapen what God is doing for us. The best we can do is walk along-side of others, offering a quiet grace on the journey.

Journeying with Others in Grace

Parker Palmer, the well-known author, teacher and speaker, writes a time when he was clinically depressed: "I could feel nothing except the burden of my own life and the exhaustion, the apparent futility of trying to sustain it" (Palmer, 2000, p. 58). Counselors who have worked with depressed cli-ents—and those who have themselves experienced depression—under-stand something of Palmer's description. Depression is like a thick, dark fog that envelops a human soul and makes each new day a tentative and uncertain drudgery.

Palmer writes of his visitors. All of them meant well, but only a few were able to minister to him in the depth of his pain. In reading his account, I cannot help but notice the similarity between his advisors and various approaches to counseling. Some of Palmer's visitors tried to cheer him up by reminding him of the good things surrounding him. There are so many beautiful things to be appreciated in creation—the fragrance of fresh flowers, the warmth of sunshine, the beauty of rolling hills, the glory of a hearty smile. But when enclosed in a fog of depression, it feels trite and oppressive to have someone mimic Bobby McFerrin's 1980s song "Don't Worry, Be Happy." I sometimes see this same tendency in beginning counselors, trying to convince a depressed client to feel better by looking at the bright side of life. Cognitive therapists are particularly prone to this when we use our thought-bending techniques to help a client see the world more positively without first entering into the depth of their pain and struggle. The most effective cognitive therapists balance their use of techniques with attention to present feelings, circumstances and relational patterns (Jones & Pulos, 1993).

Other visitors tried to encourage Palmer by pointing out his many good qualities, affirming him for his amazing abilities and the ways he had helped so many others. But through the cloud of depression, this all felt disingenuous. Palmer filtered every good his friends mentioned through the grid of his depression and ended up with a sense of falseness. His friends meant to remind him of his strengths, but he ended up feeling like an imposter. Again, I think of some approaches to counseling, especially those that attempt to build a client's self-esteem by offering affirmations and words of encouragement. I wonder how often these counseling methods end up feeling shallow and vapid to folks in the grip of incredible pain.

A third group of visitors attempted to empathize by using the words that every counselor has regretted using: "I know just how you feel." No, we do not know how another feels. We can never fully know. Each person is comprised of a unique combination of biological, psychological, spiritual, volitional and social influences. Our uniqueness makes us mysterious, reminding us of God's incredible creativity in creation. The counselor who learns only to parrot a client's pain and to offer only reflective words of understanding may have an unintended effect. Palmer laments, "Paradoxically, it was my friends' empathetic attempt to identify with me that made me feel even more isolated, because it was overidentification. Disconnection may be hell, but it is better than false connections" (Palmer, 2000, p. 62).

Thankfully, some of Palmer's visitors understood the mystery of companionship in the midst of human suffering. One of his friends, Bill, came each afternoon to massage Palmer's feet. Bill would sit in near silence, speaking only an occasional word, while offering human touch and comfort to a sacred soul with weary feet. I am not suggesting that counselors peel off their clients' shoes and socks and offer foot rubs for $120 per hour; indeed, licensing boards and supervisors would have legitimate concerns with such practices! But there is something in the rhythm of Bill interacting with Parker that is reminiscent of good counseling. It is one human being sitting with another, being present in a time of darkness, offering a ministry of mercy while avoiding trite words of advice or comfort. Bill's is not a shallow "I-know-how-you-feel" sort of empathy, but a companionate empathy where two people sit together and acknowledge how difficult life in a broken world can be. But as they sit together in a posture of sorrow, there is a glimmer of hope because, however sorrowful they may be, they are still sitting together, enveloped in a common faith that God is good even in the darkest moments of life. Hope may be found in a steady thumb caressing a calloused foot, in a timely smile, in a simple prayer offered by one for the sake of the other or in a word of compassion. Our world is broken, terribly broken—God knows—but it is not shattered. Creation is still good, God is still active, Christ is still sustaining our world (Col 1:17). And so there is love and hope and faith, and where they all intersect there is the possibility of grace.

In his book *Addiction and Grace,* Gerald May (1988) admitted that he could not define or describe grace adequately; the closest he could come was to describe images of grace. Ultimately, grace is mystery, bigger and more powerful than words. If we have eyes to see, we find images of grace sparkling all through God's creation, helping us understand something of this mystery. They are often relational images. Parker Palmer's friend Bill is an image of grace, speaking the language of divine love without talking much at all. Palmer concludes:

> This kind of love does not reflect the "functional atheism" we sometimes practice—saying pious words about God's presence in our lives but believing, on the contrary, that nothing good is going to happen unless we make it happen. [This is] a kind of love that neither avoids nor invades the soul's suffering. It

---

SURVEY SAYS 3.1: Emissaries of Grace

Many of the Christian leaders we surveyed emphasized the importance of grace, both justifying and sanctifying. These leaders remind us that the power for change resides in Christ and not in the counselor.

> Even though we are bent by [sin] we are not definitively constrained. There is power for change toward our original design available in and through Christ's healing work and presence. Jesus is the only one who can completely release a person from the guilt of sin.
>
> God is the one that forgives and heals. He can use a wide variety of methods but ultimately it is him, and he does not choose to work the same every time.

We are merely emissaries of God's grace, fully revealed in the life and work of Jesus. Christ is the one who works in us and through us.

"My old self has been crucified with Christ. It is no longer I who live, but Christ lives in me. So I live in this earthly body by trusting in the Son of God, who loved me and gave himself for me. I do not treat the grace of God as meaningless" (Gal 2:20-21).

---

is a love in which we represent God's love to a suffering person, a God who does not "fix" us but gives us strength by suffering with us. By standing respectfully and faithfully at the borders of another's solitude, we may mediate the love of God to a person who needs something deeper than any human being can give. (Palmer, 2000, p. 64)

People often ask what makes Christian counseling Christian. Perhaps Palmer, who is not a counselor, has hinted at an answer. A Christian counselor believes that healing goes beyond what a human can offer. Instead, we hope to be mediators of God's grace to those who seek our services.

There is a strangely seductive power that Christian counselors must ward off; it is the belief that we ourselves are the engineers of healing: *we* gain the graduate degrees, *we* derive the theories of counseling, *we* establish healing relationships with our clients, *we* deliver the treatment and monitor progress. Surely *we* must be the ones who care for and cure the souls entrusted to us. But there is a substantial difference between being a mediator of God's healing presence and being the source of healing. Christian counselors recognize that they are not the source; they are emissaries of God's healing grace. In the context of a quiet grace, surrounded by the love of God and the care of a competent counselor, clients find the safety to *discover* their sinfulness and the wounds of living in a sinful world. And then they find the courage to *recover* under the sanctifying power of grace, becoming more and more like the fully functioning humans that were last seen near a fruit grove in Eden.

4

Holding Sin and Grace Together—
Three Perspectives

WHEN I WAS ASKED TO DEMONSTRATE Christian counseling for the American Psychological Association's Psychotherapy Video Series, I had two responses. The first was, "But no one, including me, seems to know what Christian counseling is!" The second reply—which came only a few seconds later—was, "Sure, I'll do it." After saying yes I had several months to ponder my fate before showing up in the studio to tape the session (McMinn, 2006). It occurred to me that I better have some way of understanding and explaining Christian counseling before showing up. I had been a Christian psychologist for many years, but I still had difficulty wrapping my thoughts and words around the diffuse movement known as Christian counseling. Ultimately, I decided the term is used so differently by various groups that I could not attempt to offer a single definition. Some Christian counselors offer psychoanalytic interpretations while others engage their clients in healing prayers. Some confront demons while others confront irrational beliefs. Some are licensed professionals and others are lay counselors. Some seek symptom reduction while others pursue character change. When Jon Carlson, the interviewer, asked me what Christian counseling is, I muttered that it means various things to various groups. I then went on to offer what I think it ought to mean.

Three Perspectives
Responsible Christian counseling needs three perspectives—psychology, theology and spirituality (McMinn, 1996). Just as an effective tripod needs all three legs to function, Christian counselors need these three dimensions to reach the deepest needs of people who seek our help. Psychology provides a good deal of scientific support for particular interventions and helps

us understand how people change. Theology provides a worldview that shapes our view of people, the nature of God, the work of Christ and much more. Christian spirituality reminds us that we are pilgrims on a journey, seeking to grow in Christ and become more like the people God created us to be.

Because I am trained as a psychologist—one who studies behavior and mental processes—it is inevitable that I value psychology. It is a vast discipline, ranging from basic science to highly applied work. Though all psychologists value both research and theory, their actual work varies along the continuum shown in figure 4.1. On the basic science end of the continuum, psychology is a research-based discipline in much the same way as the natural sciences (biology, physiology, biochemistry and related disciplines). For example, I had acquaintances in graduate school who studied goldfish retinas in order to better understand color vision. The basic research on this end of the continuum helps us understand behavior and mental processes through scientific inquiry. On the other end of the continuum, psychologists are engaged in highly applied work, such as counseling, psychotherapy, consulting and so on. These psychologists also value research—or at least they ought to—but their day-to-day work is based on the theory that emerges from scientific research (and other influences) more than the research itself. This applied end of the psychology continuum is often disparaged by Christian critics of psychology.

Psychologists deserve some criticism for their applied work, both because applied work often drifts away from its scientific moorings and because we easily underestimate how much our psychological theories are based in metaphysics as well as science (Jones, 1994; O'Donahue, 1989). Consider any major counseling theory—psychoanalytic, existential, hu-

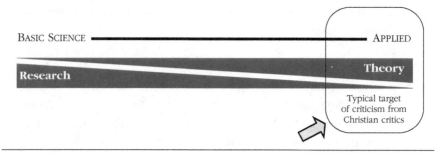

Figure 4.1. Science and application in psychology

COUNSELING TIP 4.1: *Stay Current*

In chapter one I suggested that some Christian counselors reject biblical counseling without ever reading what the biblical counselors have to say (see , for example, Counseling Tip 1.1). It is important for Christian counselors to stay current with biblical and theological studies as well as the biblical counseling literature. Of course, this works the other way around too. Some biblical counselors, and more than a few Christian counselors, seem convinced that everything they need to know is in the Bible and Christian literature, and so they neglect keeping up with psychological research. This approach minimizes the importance of science, and sometimes results in devastating consequences for clients. If a counselor fails to recognize signs of autism in a young child, for example, the child may not be referred for the intensive behavioral management treatment that can make the difference between severe impairment or relatively normal functioning as an adult. Similarly, a counselor who does not stay current with the psychological research may not realize the importance of breathing training and interoceptive exposure when treating clients with panic disorder. A treatment that could be completed in six-to-ten weeks might stretch on for months or years if the counselor does not understand the proper treatment procedures.

---

manistic, behavioral, cognitive-behavioral and so on—and one will find various worldview assumptions that are related and unrelated to scientific discoveries.

Christian counselors need not accept every theory and application that comes out of psychology, but many of the scientific and theoretical advances in psychology are worth considering. I have often wished that seminary students were required to take an introductory psychology course—taught from a theistic perspective—to better understand the wonders and brokenness of our human condition. Psychology's theories and research findings need to be evaluated with thoughtful theological reflection, but once the worldview issues are worked out, findings from psychology help us understand ourselves and others.

Psychology is helpful, but it is not fully sufficient for Christian counseling. We cannot get a full Christian understanding of helping others without also looking at theology and spirituality. It may seem confusing that I distinguish between Christian theology and spirituality. Aren't they the same thing? Perhaps they ought to be the same (some theologians would argue so), but theology and spirituality have come to have different meanings to most Christians.

In order to distinguish between Christian theology and spirituality, I must digress slightly to introduce Seymour Epstein's (1994) cognitive-experiential self theory. Epstein suggests that we all have two systems, or ways of knowing, that operate simultaneously. One is the cognitive system, which functions by analysis and logic, and the other is the experiential system, which functions more intuitively and is based on the stories and experiences of life. Imagine going to eat at a restaurant, looking at the menu and trying to decide what to order. The cognitive system will have certain analytical perspectives:

"The stroganoff costs more than the chicken."
"The chicken has fewer grams of fat."

The experiential system will be operating simultaneously but looking at the decision from a "storied" vantage point:

"Oh, the stroganoff here is to die for."
"The chicken here is fine, but nothing like what my grandmother used to make."

Or imagine looking at a bag of candy. On the front side of the bag, in large letters, the M&M's® logo activates the experiential system as you anticipate the pleasurable taste and perhaps recall previous times when M&M's® tasted so very good. But if the bag is turned over where the ingredients and nutritional information are listed, then the rational system is required to evaluate the caloric content, the various artificial ingredients and so on.

Jonathan Edwards (1746/1996), the eighteenth-century American theologian, made a similar distinction between understanding and inclination. Understanding is a cognitive capacity that allows us to "discern, see, and judge things" (p. 6). Inclination is more experiential, allowing us to feel pleasure or displeasure. We think of understanding as residing in one's head and inclination in one's heart. Our head might understand that M&M's® are somewhat unhealthy to eat, and yet our heart pulls us toward the vending machine. The distance between the head and the heart often seems much greater than twelve inches.

It's not that one system is good and the other bad—we need both to function. Our heart brings joy, spontaneity and celebration. Our head brings discernment, analysis and reason. It is also not the case that men are analytical and women experiential. Both men and women experience both ways of knowing, though certain individuals may emphasize and use one more than the other.

The point of this digression is that theology tends to emphasize our understanding about God—cognitive and intellectual—while spirituality is more about our inclination toward God—storied and experienced. Theology rigorously engages the intellect in understanding the divine, and spirituality meets us where we live and can never be contained in ivory towers. Though we would all wish for theology and spirituality to have a synergistic effect on Christian living, each strengthening the other, it sometimes does not work out so neatly. For example, in *A Cry for Mercy,* Henri Nouwen (1981) writes: "I often wonder if my knowledge about God has not become my greatest stumbling block to my knowledge of God" (p. 127). Nouwen suggests that too much reliance on the intellectual study of God can injure our personal connection with God; theology without spirituality becomes a sterile, impersonal intellectual endeavor. The converse is also problematic: spirituality without theology puts us on an experiential journey without direction. We need theological roots if we are to grow in Christian spirituality.

Each of these perspectives—psychology, theology and spirituality—helps us understand the significance of holding sin and grace together. *Psychology* helps us see that every person wrestles with defensiveness. Direct confrontation is rarely helpful in exposing defenses; a gentle, relational approach that resembles grace is more effective. *Theology* provides the most direct and authoritative glimpse of human nature, reminding us that sin is our most fundamental problem and grace our great hope. This means that Christian counseling cannot be only about helping people feel better; growth in grace and truth are also important. *Spirituality* is about the journey of life and faith, causing us to face the truth about our lonely condition. Over and over, the spiritual life calls us to confess our need for God and fall into arms of grace. Spiritually sensitive counseling can be an important part of the journey toward peace with self, God and others.

Psychology and the Language of Defense

An important concept in contemporary psychotherapy is the notion of personal defenses (see Counseling Tip 3.1). Though the concept comes from early psychoanalytic writings, it has now been generalized to almost every system of psychotherapy. We live behind armor, protecting ourselves from painful realities with selective forms of self-deception. When bad things happen, we explain them to ourselves. Most often, we explain things in ways that take blame off ourselves and place it onto others. This is true for the big things in life—such as divorce, crime, war and disease—and the little nuisances as well. I recall carrying a cup of hot chocolate up a populated stairway when I tripped and distributed my beverage all over the stairs, the wall, my clothing and my pride. Undoubtedly, my students enjoyed the moment more than I. As I was driving home to change my clothes, I found all sorts of creative explanations for my folly. If the person behind me hadn't been coming up the stairs so fast, I might not have felt so much pressure to move quickly, and I never would have tripped. Maybe it was his fault. If my new shoes didn't have these thick, bulky soles, then I would have kept my footing. Maybe it was the fault of whomever manufacturers Dockers shoes. If they didn't make the hot chocolate so hot or the paper cups so thin, then I would have concentrated on walking instead of how hot my hand felt. Maybe the fault belonged to Starbucks. In all these explanations I was protecting myself from the truth. My accusatory thoughts served as armor to keep me from the embarrassment of falling and making a mess in front of my students.

Defenses function in the bigger matters of life also. Most of us, if we are honest, believe life would be better if those around us would change. Sometimes we are right; others do need to change. Sometimes we deceive ourselves because it is we who need to change. Most of the time it is a combination of both, but we are much more prone to see fault in others than in ourselves.

Many different sorts of defenses have been labeled and defined by psychologists, and are now popularized through self-help books and public discourse. Clinical psychologists distinguish between primary (or primitive) defenses, which pertain to the relationship of a person to the outer world, and more mature defenses, which relate to internal psychological processes (McWilliams, 1994). Denial is an example of a primitive defense, because a person in denial refuses to accept some objective state of reality. For example, a person guilty of rape may believe that his date actually wanted to have sex. Other primitive defenses include projection (attributing one's faults or errors to someone else, such as in my hot chocolate episode), splitting (viewing others as either perfect or awful) and withdrawal (retreating into a fantasy world rather than dealing with the complexities of interpersonal interactions). More sophisticated defenses include repression (motivated forgetting of painful events), regression (retreating to an earlier state of development when faced with stress), intellectualization (dealing with pain by confining it to logical analysis) and rationalization (coming up with a "good explanation" to excuse one's faults).

Defenses are not limited to clinical work and the applied end of the continuum in figure 4.1. The subdisciplines hovering closer to the basic science end of the continuum, such as social and cognitive psychology, have also discovered defensive processes. For example, we quite naturally seek out information that is consistent with what we already believe: we tend to filter new information through our beliefs rather than forming beliefs based on the information, and we persevere in our beliefs even when given contrary evidence. These forms of defense will be discussed more in later chapters.

Religion can also be defensive. It is quite common to encounter those who use faith-based clichés to keep from exploring the painful existential questions of life and death. Many Christians hide behind feel-good verses such as Romans 8:28 ("And we know that God causes everything to work together for the good of those who love God and are called according to his purpose for them") without also acknowledging the angst Paul described a few verses earlier in Romans 8:20-23 (we groan and struggle in this fallen world).

The point of psychological maturity is to gain a more honest look at ourselves in relation to others; Christian maturity is about gaining a more honest look at ourselves and others in relation to God. In both cases, this requires gradual discovery and releasing of our defensive styles. How is this accomplished? Experienced counselors will note that helping people understand defensive processes is slow and tedious work that requires an enormous amount of gentleness and rapport between the client and counselor. If anyone ever writes a book called *Psychotherapy for Dummies,* one of the chapter titles should be "Don't Confront Defenses Too Soon." People wear armor for a reason, and it takes a good deal of trust and safety before they are willing to take it off.

Our self-delusions die slowly. It takes time to tell ourselves the truth. We have to sift through all our impulses for self-protection before we can

IN THE OFFICE 4.1: Guilt as Defense

Guilt can be a useful and productive emotion because it leads to contrition and renewed efforts to change (see In the Office 2.3). But it is important to recognize a defensive function in guilt also. Those who become convicted about a recurrent problem and gain new motivation to change are often at risk of dropping out of counseling prematurely because they are so encouraged and inspired by the desire to change. Wanting to change is not the same as changing! Counselors need to watch for this.

Melissa: This can be our last session. I've finally kicked this problem.

Mark: Wow. You've had an encouraging week!

Melissa: Yes, I really have. Over the weekend I had a breakthrough. I was praying about how out of control I feel sometimes, and I sensed God's comfort and closeness in a new and fresh way. And every day since it has been the same. I've had no urges to binge, and I'm eating well.

Mark: That sounds like an incredible experience. Fill me in a bit. What was going on over the weekend that led up to that time of prayer?

Melissa: Well, Friday night was bad. I came home from work and just started eating, and the next thing I knew I was out of control. It was one of the worst binges ever. I purged, and then the same thing happened later that night. I went to bed feeling terrible. But Saturday morning, I was lying in bed praying, and I experienced this incredible peace from God.

Mark: What a gift, that deep awareness of God's love and presence.

Melissa: It was amazing.

Mark: You also mentioned that you feel like you've kicked the eating disorder and can stop counseling now. Tell me more about that.

There is no need or reason to question Melissa's profound experience of God's comfort, but her desire to stop counseling—fueled by the defensive nature of her guilt and the power of forgiveness she later experienced—is premature. Despite Melissa's powerful spiritual experience, a few days of healthy eating does not mean that a five-year problem with an eating disorder is cured.

understand how we are part of the problem. In early adulthood I spent a year in personal therapy; I will always recall one conversation that changed everything. After spending much of our session bemoaning that no one really understood me, that others didn't love me for who I was, that people used my goodwill for their own advantage, I expected the therapist's usual kind, compassionate, reflective response. Perhaps she would look at me and say, "Oh that sounds so painful, Mark." Or maybe she would say, "I see how much you are longing to feel valued and understood by those you care about." We therapists are trained in this sort of thing. But she didn't say anything of the sort. She looked me directly in the eye and said, "That sounds like a narcissistic fantasy to me."

I immediately felt misunderstood, ashamed and even a bit betrayed. I wanted fig leaves. But then I looked in the eyes of my therapist, who was grandmotherly both in age and in her kind disposition, and saw the compassion and mercy she had always offered me. This woman meant me no harm; she was guiding me toward the truth. And her words began to seep down through my defenses.

My therapist's stark statement of truth—which I could hear only because of the grace she had shown in earlier sessions—became the turning point of my personal therapy. It helped me see how much I am like everyone else: broken, longing for love, prone to blame, yearning to be understood, yet self-deceived and desperate for mercy. I wanted my therapist to collude with me in blaming others for the pain in my life. She gave me a much greater gift: a growing awareness of my brokenness in the context of a gracious therapy relationship.

Theology and the Language of Truth and Grace

Along with Karl Barth and other dialectic theologians, I am compelled by John 1:14: "The Word became flesh and made his dwelling among us. We have seen his glory, the glory of the one and only Son, who came from the Father, full of grace and truth" (TNIV). Here we see both the essence and mystery of the gospel, indeed the essence and mystery of the Bible and of all history. God is transcendent—residing above creation—but is not limited to transcendence. God chooses to be known, to be made tangible, in order to cure our sinful souls. Developmental psychologists who study childhood spirituality often have children draw a picture of God—this helps the psychologist understand something of who the child perceives God to be. Jesus is the perfect picture of God, the "visible image of the invisible God" (Col 1:15). When John describes the *Logos,* the eternal Word, as full of grace and truth, he is drawing a picture of God.

Sometimes it seems that people are good at one or the other—either grace or truth—and that finding balance is difficult. Christianity calls us to both. In chapter one, I argued that it is silly to divide the Christian counseling world into those who emphasize sin and those who emphasize grace. In the same way, we cannot separate truth and grace into distinct personality characteristics or counseling strategies. To make such a distinction does injustice to the character of God revealed in Christ. Grace and truth are complementary constructs, inextricably connected.

The word for truth used in John 1:14 is not so much about honest expression as it is about faithfulness. Just as a wall is "true" if it is perfectly straight, so also Jesus is completely faithful, virtuous and righteous. The truth of God orients us to the crookedness of our own hearts and the fallen state of all creation. We cannot fully understand grace unless we understand this concept of truth, because we need truth as a frame of reference in order to distinguish mere kindness from grace. If there is no plumb line to determine what is crooked and straight, then kindness is the best we can hope for and there is no need for grace. If there are no transcendent properties of truth operating in our world, then nothing is off-kilter either. Counseling becomes a place to express human acceptance and compassion as a client explores memories, events and relationships that have been disruptive and painful.

But if there is a standard of truth revealed in Christ, and if all of us fall short of this standard, then kindness is not enough—we need grace. We need forgiveness and unconditional love to cure our crooked souls, and not just a compassionate companion through the unpredictable journey of life. Grace—merciful kindness expressed to those who can never deserve it—is a quality God offers. Those committed to following Christ strive to become messengers of his grace, whether in the counseling office or somewhere else.

To the Christian who accepts the notion of transcendent truth, counseling and every other process of personal and spiritual growth is ultimately dependent on God's grace. It may be common grace, functioning beneath the threshold of awareness for counselor and client, but it is still God's doing. Christian counseling recognizes that God is at work everywhere, whether or not God's creatures acknowledge it.

SURVEY SAYS 4.1: Confession and Grace

The Christian leaders my students and I surveyed noted the importance of confession in the life of a Christian. Without exception, every comment we received about confession was coupled with an awareness of God's grace or freedom.

> Freedom can come through repentance.
>> When we sin, we need to go through the humbling process of confessing, repenting, receiving forgiveness and also experiencing grace.
>> We must continually pray for deeper awareness of our sin, the necessity of repentance and the wonderful gift of grace that is never ending.

God does not desire us to wallow in shame, but to turn from our self-deceived ways and to seek a new and better way of living. God, who desires reconciliation, calls us to confess that we are sinners so that we may establish a new hope and identity in the grace and truth of Christ.

People in the grips of sin used to visit a priest to confess that their behavior had been off-kilter, failing to match the plumb line of God's truth. The priest might suggest some form of penance to help the person acknowledge the weight of sin, but then the priest would offer an enormous gift—God's grace and reconciliation. Today we go to the psychotherapist, from whom we learn that our behavior is understandable, the product of our parents' conduct or our spouse's need for control. Or perhaps our behavior is a symptom of a chemical imbalance. Sometimes we may exchange the language of grace and truth for the language of self-esteem and positive self-talk. As a practicing psychologist, I believe in the value of psychotherapy. It is good to explore parent-child relationships, look for biological explanations and understand dysfunctional family relationships. But none of these things should dismiss the language of grace and truth. We're all caught in the midst of a sinful world that manifests itself in our biology and our close relationships as much as our willful choices. Our greatest hope is going through the long, slow process of understanding our crookedness, acknowledging our part in the problem, then seeking reconciliation with God and one another.

If we lean toward a graceless view of truth, suggesting that counseling is little more than identifying moral failings, we are partly right, of course, because our character has all sorts of implications for physical and psychological health. Even mainstream psychologists are interested in how virtuous living enhances mental health (Peterson & Seligman, 2004). But such a view can easily become presumptuous and insensitive if offered in a spirit of condescension. All humanity—including pastors and Christian counselors—is broken, so even the best biblical exegetes, philosophers, pastors and Christian counselors are unable to properly discern truth in some situations. Further, it is misleading and offensive to reduce psychological problems to simplistic cause-and-effect algorithms because the complexity of human problems defies simple solutions, whether the problems are sociological (such as institutional racism or divorce rates), economic (such as global hunger or warming) or psychological (such as depression or addiction). All of us function in the complexity of a crooked world, hindered by our own sin, the sin of others and the fallen state of created order. We need to work together in merciful companionship to help one another see things straight, and we need the sanctifying grace of God to help us move toward greater truth.

Or we can lean too far in the other direction, toward a truthless view of grace. It is easy to lean this way because there is incredible beauty in the incarnation, God becoming flesh to come live among us in our squalor. It is compelling and amazing, and it inspires us to also sit in quiet grace with those in the midst of messy life situations. This is a noble inclination—one that every Christian counselor and pastor should embrace. And not only Christians aspire to this. I noted when Gerald Koocher, then president of the American Psychological Association and a man of Jewish background, wrote a column about sitting for two hours with a dying woman (Koocher, 2006). After she died her family members gave Koocher a five-word note the patient had written in her final moments of life: "Thank you for being there." Being *there* is exactly where we ought to be, inspired by Mother Teresa, Gerald Koocher and Parker Palmer's friend, Bill, who showed up to massage Parker's feet every day during his time of depression (Palmer, 2000). I have noticed a trend these days to refer to this as "incarnational" living, which I admire insofar as it reminds us of the incredible grace of Christ and our human desire to follow in that example. But we must be cautious, too, because there was only one incarnation and it occurred when "the Word became flesh and made his dwelling among us . . . full of grace *and truth*" (Jn 1:14 TNIV). Jesus made truth claims. He insisted that some values were better than

---

IN THE OFFICE 4.2: Respecting Autonomy Without Agreeing

An ethical principle of virtually all counseling professions is that counselors respect their clients' autonomy. Counselees have the right to believe as they choose, even if contrary to their counselors' beliefs. Counselors who are unwilling to respect their clients' autonomy should choose another profession where persuasion is a more overt and explicit part of their work. But respecting a client's autonomy is not the same as agreeing with whatever the client says. For example:

> Ben: It's important to me that Liz and I live together for a while before we get married, just to see if we're compatible. I don't understand why her parents are all freaked out about it.

Counselor A	**Counselor B**
I see what you mean. It is important to you to be sure about Liz before you get married. And living together is the way you would like to see that happen.	Getting to know Liz well before marriage is an important value to you. What sort of values are her parents trying to communicate?

Counselor A may not be intending to agree with the client, but the client will hear agreement. Counselor B is respecting the client's autonomy while encouraging an exploration of other values. Sometime later Counselor B may express personal or doctrinal disagreement with Ben's plan, but it will be within the context of a caring and grace-filled relationship that also respects Ben's right to autonomy. When Christian counselors confuse autonomy and agreement they inadvertently communicate that truth is relative and self-defined. They end up compromising truth in the name of grace.

---

others. He confronted religious leaders. He even called them names on occasion. Jesus, the eternal Word, became flesh and dwelled among us, because there is a standard of truth that needed to be honored and revealed to humanity, something more than just sitting with us in our pain. And so Christian counseling, if it is indeed Christian, must be founded on basic assumptions of truth.

It is important for counselors to consider the nature of truth that Christ revealed. Not only did Jesus come to teach truth but also to be truth in our midst—to reveal God's intention for humankind. For centuries spiritual directors have discussed the true and false self; Jesus was a perfectly true self. Christ is the only whole and completely true person to ever walk on our planet. God's desire is that we become more like Jesus, journeying toward our true selves—fully connected to God and neighbor (Benner, 2005).

This does not mean that we preach to our clients, because counseling is different than preaching, but it does mean that when we sit with others in the messiness and pain of life, we reflect a hope that is even bigger than human companionship. It is a hope that truth is worth knowing, though we see it through a glass dimly, and virtue worth seeking. It is a hope that someday all will again be set straight.

Spirituality and the Problem of Loneliness

Life outside of Eden is a lonely endeavor. Many times the loneliness of living lies beneath the anxiety, anger, depression and addiction we see in our counseling offices. A doctrine of sin helps us understand the causes of loneliness, and a doctrine of grace gives us hope to keep journeying toward greater awareness of God's good purposes and persistent love.

Loneliness is a paradox of contemporary life. On one hand, technological advances make it virtually inconceivable that one could ever be lonely. Almost every residence in the developed world has one or more telephones, enabling us to stay in touch with friends and family anywhere in the world. And now we have cellular phones so that we can stay in touch while riding the commuter train or sitting at a stoplight or standing in the grocery store line. Those who have no one to call can get online and find a chat room filled with others eager to participate in conversation and who knows what else. Even the Luddites among us are likely to own a television, with its ceaseless drone of drama, humor, talk and so-called television personalities. On the other hand, the technology that provides us with so many relational options may simultaneously rob us of the simple interpersonal blessings that could be part of everyday life. The conveniences offered by garage door openers and air conditioners also prevent us from stepping outside where we might encounter others who inhabit the houses next door. Rather than spending a summer evening on the front porch with neighbors, the television entertains us in the family room—which rarely contains the whole family (some households may have two or three televisions operating in distinct rooms so that everyone can maintain control over their viewing options).

Rather than chatting with a new acquaintance in the grocery store line, we are left to endure the person three feet in front of us yelling into a cellular phone. Instead of being known fully by a person committed to a lasting relationship, many seem content to try on new personalities in a chat room, never knowing for sure who they are chatting with on the other side of cyberspace. We live isolated and alone in our comfort.

But I fear I have jumped onto a contemporary bandwagon in blaming technology for our loneliness. The gadgets contribute, of course, but I wonder if the problem may run deeper, saturating the very essence of modernity, free-market economies and contemporary lifestyles. Everywhere I go in the developed world I encounter people with too much to do and not enough time to do it. We hustle around thinking busyness is a virtue that helps us

---

COUNSELING TIP 4.2: *Loneliness and the Pornography Crisis*

Christian men and women everywhere are confronting problems with compulsive pornography use. In response, we tell people to just say no. Stop viewing explicit sexual images on the Internet. Stop renting inappropriate videos. Stop viewing certain magazines. Of course this is all good advice, but with all our effort to restrain inappropriate behavior we sometimes forget to enhance appropriate behavior. People turn to pornography because they feel an inner ache of loneliness that persists despite their real-life relationships. They seek to patch things up with a sexual thrill, but the end result is just more shame and secrecy and isolation. Counseling those with pornography problems is not just a matter of getting them to stop bad behaviors; it is also a process of helping them encounter their loneliness and to develop new patterns of relating to God and others in honest and healthy ways.

---

accomplish what really matters, though we are not particularly good at articulating what it is that matters so very much. When I sit alone in my family room on Sunday afternoon, watching an NFL team move into a hurry-up offensive as they fall frantically behind near the end of the game, I am reminded of the way many of us live most days. In a competitive, hurry-up world it is difficult to know and be known. Nouwen (1972) wrote about this more than thirty years ago. "We live in a society in which loneliness has become one of the most painful human wounds. The growing competition and rivalry which pervade our lives from birth have created in us an acute awareness of our isolation" (p. 83).

Still, I think my analysis fails to plumb the depths of human loneliness. Technology adds to our isolation, and living in a competitive world does too, but I suspect there is something even deeper that the existentialists and Christian mystics have seen. Nouwen's point is not so much that contemporary living has made us lonely, but that it makes us aware that life outside Eden is always tinged with loneliness. Perhaps it is not so important that we identify the contemporary locus of our loneliness as that we begin to acknowledge we are naturally lonely, isolated by our state of sin as surely as by our garage door openers and free-market economy. In the words of Ronald Rolheiser (1999), a Catholic theologian:

> When we fail to mourn properly our incomplete lives then this incompleteness becomes a gnawing restlessness, a bitter center, that robs our lives of all delight. Because we do not mourn . . . we demand that someone or something— a marriage partner, a sexual partner, an ideal family, having children, an achievement, a vocational goal, or a job—take all of our loneliness away. That, of course, is an unreal expectation, which invariably leads to bitterness and disappointment. In this life, there is no finished symphony. We are built for the infinite, Grand Canyons without a bottom. Because of that we will, this side of eternity, always be lonely, restless, incomplete . . . living in the torment of the insufficiency of everything attainable. (p. 157)

It all seems quite dire as long as we insist on fixing the loneliness. But once loneliness is accepted as a natural and inevitable consequence of living in a fallen world we can stop fighting the pain and look for signs of joy and hope along life's journey.

The author of Hebrews, in describing various Old Testament heroes of faith, notes, "They agreed that they were foreigners and nomads here on earth" (Heb 11:13). When I give devotionals on this passage I tend to emphasize the "foreigners and nomads" phrase, but maybe the more significant point is that "they agreed." We need to admit our condition, to agree with one another that life is often lonely and sad and difficult, that the ultimate problem is spiritual estrangement as much as psychological disorder, and that our greatest hope is brighter than what selective serotonin reuptake inhibitors or psychotherapy can ever offer (though, thankfully, we have these palliative means of care available).

A life without acknowledging sin is a dismal proposition insofar as it leaves people in a quandary as to why life is so difficult, relationships so challenging and meaning so elusive. Christian spirituality offers an answer. It is a difficult answer, but an answer nonetheless. We journey on an arduous path because of the profound contaminating effects of sin in our fallen world. And once we have that settled and lower our expectations accordingly, then we can begin to see the simple pleasure and beauty of this journey. As long as we expect an easy journey we are bound for disappointment and discouragement, but once we accept the inevitability of loneliness, doubt and fear we free ourselves to be surprised by joy.

Though tainted by sin, creation is still beautiful and good. The spiritual journey is not only about struggle and loneliness; it also reveals God's creativity and bounty—divine love revealed in a blossoming flower or a glistening glade of grass moistened by the dew of a new day. Sure enough, the grubs and aphids eat away at botanical beauty, but what beauty it is! Everywhere we look there is hope and the promise that God still loves this broken world and is actively involved in redeeming it. Yes, we are lonely—no human relationship satisfies every desire—but still, what incredible joy can be found in the touch and companionship of a partner, in the safe presence of a friend, in the wisdom of a teacher or mentor. Toil is mingled with hope at every point along the journey.

Every symbol of hope on the Christian journey points to a God who delights in us and promises a day when God's glory will be fully revealed in every moment of every day. After describing those heroes of faith that "agreed that they were foreigners and nomads here on earth" (Heb 11:13), the author of Hebrews goes on: "Obviously people who say such things are looking forward to a country they can call their own. If they had longed for the country they come from, they could have gone back. But they were looking for a better place, a heavenly homeland. That is why God is not ashamed to be called their God, for he has prepared a city for them" (Heb 11:14-16). We get glimpses of God's grace now, but Christians look forward to a day when splendor of God's love is unrestrained. Jonathan Edwards put it so beautifully in a sermon delivered in 1738:

> There the Holy Spirit shall be poured forth with perfect sweetness, as a pure river of water of life, clear as crystal . . . a river whose waters are without any manner of pollution. And every member of that glorious society shall be without blemish of sin or imprudence or any kind of failure. The whole church

shall then be presented to Christ as a bride clothed in fine linen . . . without spot or wrinkle. . . . In that world, wherever the inhabitants turn their eyes they shall see nothing but beauty and glory (Kimnach, Minkema & Sweeney, 1999, p. 247).

However messed up our broken world may be, the story is not over yet. The Christian narrative is ultimately a comedy and not a tragedy; it ends gloriously, with unimaginable joy. Someday, there will be a new heaven and a new earth. Birds will sing in tones and melodies we have never heard. Lions and lambs will tumble and play in grass that is a deeper green than we have ever known. Our bodies won't be riddled with wrinkles, muscle spasms and cancer. There will be pure joy and beauty and goodness. The fig leaves will be back on the trees where they belong. And God, who longs to be with us, will be our greatest joy and delight.

Conclusion

There is both good news and bad news embedded in the truth that we are all sinners. The metaphysical reality of sin is terrible—as bad as it gets. Being sinners means we are wounded, we wound others, and we live in a global community where various wounds confound and magnify small problems until they become huge problems. Sin keeps us far from God and far from one another. Sin is truly terrible.

But the truth of God—the plumb line that reveals the crookedness of fallen creation—is coupled with amazing grace. And so an awareness of sin is a good thing. Pleading guilty, admitting our fallen, broken state opens the possibility of a grace that is greater than all our sin and all our accomplishments. James Bryan Smith (1995), an author and spiritual leader, writes, "Now we can stop lying to ourselves. We are saved from our own self-deception the moment we say with the tax collector, 'God be merciful to me, *a sinner*' (Luke 18:13). We no longer need to apply cosmetics to make ourselves more acceptable to God. We have been accepted by God, and therefore, we can accept ourselves" (p. 36).

Part of our brokenness is that we turn this upside down. We are products of an era that tells us it is a bad thing to think of ourselves as sinners. We think the language of sin leads to self-hatred, judgment and criticism. So we exchange a vocabulary that brings the possibility of deep healing for cheap alternatives that offer few solutions and add to our defensiveness. We trade the deepest longing of our souls—to revel in the love of

God and in love for one another—for a therapeutic language of self-love. No wonder we feel lonely.

Once we acknowledge that our journey is made lonely by the isolating effects of sin then we can stop our frantic efforts to fix the ache of living and learn to rest in God's grace. In the safety of grace we can afford to look honestly at ourselves, experience contrition and confess our wrongdoing and the wrongs done against us. Augustine wrote in his *Confessions*, "I will now call to mind my past foulness and the carnal corruptions of my soul, not because I love them, but that I may love you, O my God" (Augustine 398/1986, p. 21).

5

Sin and Grace in Integrative Psychotherapy

DURING A THIRTEEN-YEAR TEACHING STINT AT Wheaton College in Illinois, I had the opportunity to teach alongside two outstanding biblical scholars, Walter Elwell and Gary Burge, in a course titled "Theological and Religious Issues in Psychotherapy." At first I found it intimidating because these men are so brilliant and well-informed. They understand Greek and Hebrew, study the ancient cultures from which biblical writing emerged, know about the various heresies and church councils that have punctuated Christian history, and are gifted at incisive thinking and clear communication. I recall how sloppy and amorphous my theological musings seemed alongside their precision, much like my four-year-old daughter used to look with licorice ice cream all over her face, hands, clothing and hair as I dabbed my mouth after each bite of my anything-but-licorice ice cream cone. But over time I came to realize that Walter and Gary—and the students we taught together—benefited from my psychological training as well. Psychologists encounter the messy realities of life as they sit with clients facing all sorts of struggles, challenges and pain. Such encounters do not always lend themselves to tidy formulations of propositional truth, but they help us understand the texture of life in a fallen world. Walter or Gary would often begin our classes with a succinct lecture on a particular theological topic (e.g., sin, grace, forgiveness, redemption, revelation), and then I would raise case examples that illustrated and sometimes complicated the theological precision they offered.

Counseling Is Messy Business

The situations counselors confront on a daily basis often do not fit into tidy and succinct doctrinal analyses. For example, it is utterly true that we are

---

SURVEY SAYS 5.1: The Complex Connection Between Sin and Psychopathology

Some of our survey respondents suggested that counselors need to pay more attention to sin as the cause of psychological problems. For example:

> Sin produces guilt. Guilt leads to depression, anger, etc. Jesus is the only one who can completely release a person from the guilt of sin.
>
> Sin appears to be the underlying cause of most forms of depression and many "disorders." That is, unforgiven, unresolved sin issues have psychological manifestations that are too often left untreated or masked by medication.
>
> [Sin] is the root of many of the conditions that they explain in other ways.
>
> That sin is a source for dysfunction, and that it is part of an explanation for human problems.
>
> Sin is the root cause of psychological problems.

On one hand, I have little disagreement with these assertions. As explored in chapter two, a large view of sin has tremendous explanatory power when looking at human problems. But on the other hand, I am concerned with how tidy some connections between sin and psychopathology seem to be. In my experience as a counselor, I find the connections between personal sin and psychological problems to be extremely complex. Some very mature Christians who are well along on the journey of sanctification face serious psychological problems. Others whose lives are filled with hedonism appear to function quite well psychologically. It is best not to make any quick or simplistic links between sin and psychological problems when doing counseling.

---

sinful creatures who can never reach a holy God by merit or effort; our hope is in God's grace alone, and the proper response to the grace that God lavishes on us is gratitude and praise. But what can be done to convince the husband and wife in distress that God's grace has some particular relevance for their troubled marriage? Perhaps more to the point, and more challenging, how can a counselor help them see that they are each prone to sinful and self-centered views that perpetuate problems in their marriage? Offering scriptural guidance and theological perspectives to clients may be helpful to a point, but these do not always produce affective, volitional and relational change.

Eduardo and Maria hobble into a counselor's office after many months of escalating conflict and turmoil. A year previously, Eduardo sustained a frontal-lobe head injury in an automobile accident, and Maria has noticed a substantial personality change as a result. Once easygoing and amiable, he has become withdrawn and irritable. His social judgment has become questionable. Maria recently overheard Eduardo telling a racist joke, for example, when in the past he had been highly aware of cultural diversity and human rights. He has gotten easily angered by their three young children, and he has become emotionally aloof at home. Most of the child-rearing responsibilities have fallen on Maria since the accident, and she is trying to maintain a full-time job as well. Eduardo has been able to maintain his job, but his performance reviews are declining and both Eduardo and Maria fear that he may lose his job in the near future. As a couple, they are tense around each

---

COUNSELING TIP 5.1: *Sorting the Mess*

Counseling is messy business, but sometimes a systematic approach to listening can help reduce the mess. When a client reports being overwhelmed by the stresses and demands of life, it can be helpful for the counselor and client to simply make a list of the stressors. This helps the counselor understand the complexity of the client's life, and it also helps the client sort out the mess and set priorities for what needs to be addressed first. I demonstrate this counseling strategy in a DVD on Christian counseling published by the American Psychological Association (McMinn, 2006).

---

other, arguing frequently about parenting, responsibilities around the house and financial matters. Maria feels overwhelmed by the changes she sees in Eduardo, and Eduardo has noticed that Maria has changed too. She is more tense and critical than he has ever known her to be. In the midst of several recent arguments, Maria has mentioned the word *divorce*, though she and Eduardo both see divorce as contrary to their Christian beliefs. After the most recent argument, they decided to see a Christian counselor.

There are important theological principles to consider in this situation. Both Eduardo and Maria are whole persons with biological bodies. Both are made in God's image, with amazing capacities to value goodness, treat one another with kindness and constrain their impulses. Yet they are both sinners, prone to put self-interest above the interest of the other. Both have been sinned against and they carry the scars of past offenses. And now Eduardo's body has been further compromised by a brain injury. He still has some degree of control over and responsibility for his choices but not as much as before the accident. Both Eduardo and Maria long for love and grace and stability in their relationship—because they are created for relationship—though the contours of their marriage have changed drastically since the car accident. In the midst of her distress, Maria has entertained thoughts of divorce, though she recognizes that God would have her honor her commitment and stay with Eduardo. Theologically speaking, it is important to affirm that God is still good even in the midst of the unexplained difficulties and unpredictable twists in Eduardo's and Maria's lives.

These theological parameters, and many more, are important to consider when working with Eduardo and Maria, but theology alone will likely not be sufficient in helping them through this crisis. Some Christian counselors have responded to complex situations such as this by disregarding the theological essence of their work, which is unfortunate and destructive to the cause of Christianity. At the same time many Christian leaders have retreated from the messiness of human suffering, relegating soul care to counselors who do not understand or care much about doctrinal orthodoxy. The result has been a regrettable divide between theology and psychology (Charry, 2001). A truly integrative approach to soul care must consider both.

Integrative Psychotherapy

Theoretical models are a bit like a road atlas, helping counselors figure out how to maneuver challenging clinical situations to help their clients arrive at some predetermined destination. We choose between multiple paths leading to the same end point. A behavioral therapist would help Eduardo and Maria build more positive and affirming behaviors into their marriage. They might be taught the principles of positive behavior exchanges or instructed to increase the number of pleasant events they pursue together. Cognitive therapists would help Maria and Eduardo reappraise their situation. Perhaps their troubles are worsened by the automatic thoughts they are entertaining and the underlying core beliefs that shape their day-to-day thoughts. Object relations therapists would explore early relationships to see how Maria and Eduardo may be reenacting some past relationship in their current marriage.

Some Christian counselors claim to reject all theoretical formulations derived from psychology, often because many of the major psychological theories have their roots in offensive metaphysical assumptions. But this is a bit like claiming not to breathe because the air is contaminated. It is impossible to function without guiding assumptions and beliefs that are psychological in nature. Just as theologians begin with certain presuppositions about the nature of God, humans and the world, so also counselors have a particular set of "lenses" through which they view their work. A counselor may explicitly reject all the major psychological theories, but the counselor still is operating with some sort of theoretical grid to explain behavior and mental processes (i.e., psychology), however implicit the theoretical grid may be. These guiding psychological assumptions constantly shape the words and behaviors of the counselor. Ideally, the counselor's theological presupposi-

---

COUNSELING TIP 5.2: *Articulating a Theoretical Orientation*

Professional standards require counselors to have a written informed consent form that clients review and sign at the beginning of a counseling relationship. One aspect of the consent form is a brief description of the counselor's approach. This is an excellent discipline for counselors because it requires us to define and articulate how we work. Here is an excerpt from my consent form that describes my theoretical approach:

> My approach to psychotherapy is shaped by my Christian worldview. Though I have no expectation that you share my beliefs, you have a right to know them. Christianity teaches that we are created to be in relationship with God and one another, but because of the brokenness of our world our frustrated longings for relationship often result in various problems. In this sense, psychological problems—like all problems in our world—ultimately stem from our human brokenness. However, we cannot settle for simplistic connections between personal choices and psychological symptoms. Many aspects of our fallen world contribute to psychological problems, including historical, cultural, biological, psychosocial, personal and emotional factors. Building from a foundation of a Christian worldview, my psychotherapy style involves exploring your personal history and current circumstances to identify feelings, thoughts, behaviors, assumptions, and relational patterns that contribute to your current state of distress. Both your personal values and mine will affect the process of therapy. You are free to ask for clarification about my beliefs and assumptions at any point in therapy.

tions and psychological understandings align well.

Clark Campbell and I outlined our understanding of an integrative approach to psychotherapy in a recent text, *Integrative Psychotherapy* (McMinn & Campbell, 2007). Our model draws on both psychology and theology, beginning with the belief that humans are created in the image of God. We propose three domains of intervention corresponding with three dimensions of the *imago Dei.*

Functional. Over the centuries, theologians have articulated functional, structural and relational theories of the *imago Dei,* each of which captures some essence of God's nature and some essence of human nature. Functional views emphasize that humans were created to be stewards of creation. God's charge for humans to manage the earth comes just after the *imago Dei* is introduced in Genesis 1.

> So God created human beings in his own image.
> In the image of God he created them;
> male and female he created them.

> Then God blessed them and said, "Be fruitful and multiply. Fill the earth and govern it. Reign over the fish in the sea, the birds in the sky, and all the animals that scurry along the ground." (Gen 1:27-29)

Human functioning takes many forms, ranging from collective to individual. Collectively, we are to manage our natural resources, produce and acquire food in a way that does not deplete the earth's bounty, create a degree of safety from the elements and would-be predators, and so on. Social and family units are also called to function in particular ways in order to accomplish this larger collective calling. Filling the earth and subduing it requires more than procreation; it also involves relational stability for the sake of nurturing new lives. This, in turn, calls for a degree of personal functioning that allows a person to be healthy enough to love well and work in productive ways to provide for one's family and contribute to a community.

In this range from collective to individual functioning, counselors often work at the micro level by helping individuals, couples and families function well. The functional domain of Integrative Psychotherapy focuses on managing the challenges of life, helping clients address the anxiety-, mood- and relationship-related symptoms that hinder them from experiencing the joy and goodness of God's creation. Behavioral and cognitive-behavioral models from psychology help inform the functional domain of Integrative Psychotherapy (IP).

An effective counselor will note Maria and Eduardo's loss of functioning since Eduardo's accident. He is struggling to maintain his job and to manage family responsibilities. Maria is overfunctioning to help compensate for Eduardo's losses, but she is growing increasingly frustrated and resentful in the process. Their levels of functioning need to be addressed in counseling; some sort of cognitive rehabilitation may be useful for Eduardo, and behavior exchange training may provide some relief for their marriage.

Structural. Our human ability to function as managers of ourselves and creation is only possible because we have certain structural capacities that exceed the rest of the animal kingdom (Hoekema, 1986). Humans are in charge of the pet dog rather than vice versa. This is not based on seniority or caste but on the ontology of the human person. Structural views of the *imago Dei* emphasize that humans have innate capacities that reflect the genius of God. We are rational, moral, volitional creatures with structural capacities that far exceed the rest of creation. The structural domain of IP focuses on human cognition by helping clients probe how their assumptions, values, beliefs and thoughts are connected to the troubles they experience. This shares much in common with contemporary schema-based cognitive therapy.

Maria's mention of divorce suggests certain beliefs and assumptions that she is entertaining. Perhaps she is saying to herself, "I cannot take this any more," or "This is not the man I married," or "He will never change." Although each of these beliefs may be based on a kernel of truth, they tend to inflate with time as Maria's frustration grows. Counseling can help her regain a sense of equilibrium so that she can think more calmly about the challenges she now faces. Similarly, Eduardo may be attributing his irritability and impulsiveness to the head injury exclusively and refusing to take responsibility for his actions. Again, this is based on a kernel of truth; he is a biological being, and the organ that has most to do with his biological functioning has been injured. But still, Eduardo has some human agency remaining. He may lack some of the resources that he once had to restrain impulsive thoughts and actions, but he has not lost all agency. Helping him reestablish confidence that he can make good choices and accept responsibility for poor choices will ultimately bring hope to both Eduardo and Maria.

Relational. The last century has generated a good deal of interest in relational views of the *imago Dei*. Emil Brunner and Karl Barth—so-called neo-orthodox theologians—highlighted the relational nature of the *imago Dei* in the mid-twentieth century, and many Barth and Brunner scholars

IN THE OFFICE 5.1: Probing Rather than Dismissing

Maria has been entertaining thoughts of divorce that she mentions in times of conflict with Eduardo. Many Christian counselors might have a reflexive tendency to remind Maria that Jesus taught against divorce and that the church's historic stance has been to discourage divorce. Though there may be occasions when this sort of instructional approach is helpful, more often it will be helpful to probe her thoughts rather than dismiss them as contrary to Christianity. For example:

> Maria: I'm so tired of managing everything in our home. I'm the only real parent to my children, and now I'm expected to be Eduardo's parent too. I think about divorce sometimes; I don't know if I can keep doing this.

Dismissing

Mark: Well Maria, the Bible is very clear about divorce being wrong. It's understandable that you feel tired and frustrated, but we will need to find ways other than divorce for you to cope.

Maria: I know you're right. I shouldn't be thinking like this.

Mark: Let's find some better ways for you to think.

Probing

Mark: Your thoughts about divorce seem to reflect fatigue and fear for what the future holds.

Maria: I can't imagine doing this for twenty more years.

Mark: And it's frightening to think about.

Maria: So frightening. I just don't know if I can do it.

Mark: So that's what the divorce comments are about. You feel stuck and overwhelmed, even to the point of considering something that is contrary to your values about marriage.

Maria: I don't believe in divorce—I know it's not what God wants—and I don't think I would ever leave him. But I just don't know what to do.

Mark: So that's something you and I can work on.

In both cases the counselor is exploring the structural domain with Maria, looking for her assumptions and values regarding her marriage. Simply pronouncing how Maria should be thinking tends to shut down the conversation. Probing helps Maria explore some of the thoughts and beliefs she holds that make her vulnerable to consider divorce.

have added meaningful contributions over the past several decades. More recently, prior to his untimely death, Stanley Grenz (2000) emphasized the relational nature of the *imago Dei* as revealed in the holy trinity and the incarnation.

The passage cited previously to support functional views of the *imago Dei* also contains a fascinating reference to relationality.

> So God created human beings in his own image.
> In the image of God he created them;
> *male and female he created them.*

> Then God blessed them and said, "Be fruitful and multiply. Fill the earth and govern it. Reign over the fish in the sea, the birds in the sky, and all the animals that scurry along the ground." (Gen 1:27-29, italics added)

Prior to assigning any function for newly created humans, this passage affirms the relational nature of God's grandest creature. "In the image of God he created them; *male and female he created them.*" The *imago Dei* is not something that a person possesses as an inert ontological essence, but it is manifested in the quality of interaction in relationship with others. Barth emphasized the "I-Thou" nature of the *imago Dei;* we relate to one another and to God, and thereby reflect a God who is relational, as Father, Son and Holy Spirit.

The grand metanarrative of Scripture is relational. Jesus told the story of the prodigal son (Lk 15), which has a recklessly relational father running down a dusty path to embrace a rebellious son. Like the older brother in the story, who objects to his father's lavish grace, and the religious leaders to whom Jesus told the story, we often fail to recognize the extent of God's relational passion. To Barth, John 1:14 is the lynchpin of the gospel because it shows the extent to which God will go to restore broken relationship with sinful humanity: "So the Word became human and lived here on earth among us. He was full of unfailing love and faithfulness. And we have seen his glory, the glory of the only Son of the Father."

Counselors have various relational paradigms to guide their work. The growing influence of attachment theory (Bowlby, 1990), object relations therapy and interpersonal therapy all testify to the psychological importance of relationships. The relational domain of IP focuses on the importance of relationship in helping clients change and grow.

Though Eduardo and Maria are concerned about various dimensions of their lives, it is their relational concerns that ultimately brought them for counseling. Clark Campbell, my friend and coauthor of *Integrative Psycho-therapy,* makes the point that almost every counseling client mentions an important relationship within the first few moments of the first session. Often the psychological pain people experience is an alarm system indicating some sort of relational rupture, either in the past or present. Furthermore, the therapeutic relationship itself must be considered part of the treatment in effective counseling. If counselors could simply pronounce the truth and clients changed accordingly, then counseling would consist of one or two sessions and managed care insurance companies would be delighted. But change is not so easy! It is not as simple as the words the counselor utters, but it is the nature of the counseling relationship that brings about change.

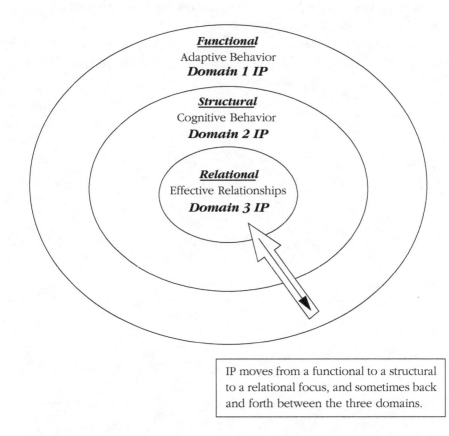

Functional
Adaptive Behavior
Domain 1 IP

Structural
Cognitive Behavior
Domain 2 IP

Relational
Effective Relationships
Domain 3 IP

IP moves from a functional to a structural to a relational focus, and sometimes back and forth between the three domains.

Figure 5.1. McMinn and Campbell's approach to Integrative Psychotherapy

A Three-Domain Approach

IP addresses all three domains—functional, structural and relational. The earliest stages of counseling lend themselves to functional matters, such as helping the client manage symptoms of distress and make strategic behavioral changes. But these changes occur in a structural context because all of us bring particular appraisals, values and beliefs to our daily functioning. Astute counselors also keep relationships in focus, because structure and function are embedded in relational and cultural contexts. Figure 5.1 shows the general direction of IP, with the functional domain commanding the most attention at first, and the structural and relational domains becoming the focus of greater attention as trust is established in the counseling relationship. Though the three domains may be seen as utterly sequential to the early therapist (i.e., start with functional interventions, then look to structural facets, then to the relationships that maintain dysfunction), more experienced counselors are able to consider the three domains simultaneously.

The Christian doctrines of sin and grace are important to consider in each domain of IP, which is the task of the three remaining chapters of this book.

6

Sin and Grace
in the Functional Domain

WAYNE IS A COLLEAGUE OF MINE AT George Fox University. In addition to being an outstanding scholar, teacher and clinician, he is an amazing gardener. To me (one who has never been able to keep a potted plant alive in his office for more than three months) a beautiful garden is a remarkable thing. I recall a brief conversation one evening as we were enjoying a lovely meal on Wayne and Nora's back deck while observing the exquisite beauty of a flower garden bursting with the colors of late spring. I asked Wayne, "Do you ever think that gardening may bring you a bit closer to Eden?" He thought so. We pondered it for a minute and then moved on to another topic. But embedded in that minute was an unspoken and humbling realization for me: all the times that I have deemed my writing and teaching and speaking to be of greater eternal significance than tending a rose bush or training clematis to climb, I have probably been wrong.

Adam and Eve were made to be stewards of a grand garden, and they were given gifts that allowed them to do so: opposable thumbs, muscular strength, endurance, creativity, intelligence, intrinsic curiosity and a love of beauty. And they were endowed with a degree of self-control so they might continue tending the garden, nurturing its potential, rather than sitting beneath a palm tree eating figs and grapes all day. It was this human capacity to function that Satan ultimately used to deceive Adam and Eve by appealing to their intrinsic curiosity and questioning their need for self-control. In a single act of rebellion, human pride was born and a beautiful creation badly distorted.

God created humans and appointed them to be functional stewards over creation, to exercise responsible control over themselves and all creation. So how are we doing? On one hand, we are doing quite well. Those who don't think so should see Wayne's garden. Human ingenuity has led to hardy hybrids, natural and chemical means of weed control, anticipating seasons and shifts in climate, and so much more. Gardening illustrates a broader reality: the human capacity to function is stunning and wondrous, reflecting the goodness of creation and the majesty of our Creator. We have harnessed various forms of energy, learned to shield ourselves from harsh winters and scorching summers, developed medicinal practices to prolong life and enhance health, discovered ways of transmitting information at remarkable speeds, and learned how to harvest all sorts of savory foods atop and beneath the earth's surface. God pronounced creation good, and it is still marvelously good.

On the other hand, in many ways we are not doing so well in our task to function as stewards over creation because all of us, and all creation, have been tainted by sin. The goodness of creation and the marvels of human functioning are undeniable, but both are fallen and tarnished. Lisa and I live in the midst of a gorgeous part of God's creation. Our abode is a country farmhouse with a wraparound porch nestled on five acres of Oregon hillside. We are surrounded with Douglas fir and oak and maple growing in the lush surrounds of the Willamette Valley. Often it seems like a bit of Eden as Lisa and I work side by side to make our land beautiful and productive. But our land, like the human heart, is infested with persistent and unpleasant weeds that we have been fighting since we first purchased the property. We are waging war with Canadian thistle, and at this point, it is not clear who is winning. It reminds us that Eden is not what it used to be. Mostly this is a metaphor for the truly bad events of the world, though Canadian thistle is quite exasperating in its own way!

Murders, health epidemics, manufacturer recalls, fires and corporate corruption all reveal that things are not right. Nations battle over ideological and political differences. Terrorists blow themselves up so they can kill a few civilians they hate. U.S. citizens enjoy an average per capita income of $34,400 while people in Ethiopia earn the equivalent of $110 (World Bank Group, 2006). One-fifth of the Earth's population uses 86 percent of its resources (Eitzen & Zinn, 2003). Basic health care is unavailable to many people, while others spend their health care dollars for things such as liposuction. Workers all over the globe are exposed to hazardous conditions in the name of profit. Mercury, lead and cadmium from our throwaway electronics become tomorrow's toxic waste. Jobs in urban centers wane as corporations follow the white flight to the suburbs. Racism lives on. So does cancer. AIDS ravages the world, especially in Africa and Asia. Pollution, urban poverty and crime threaten the great cities of the world. The world's prisons are full. Sexual harassment plagues the workplace and sneaks in the back door of our houses of worship. Illegal drugs make a few wrongfully wealthy while gripping many more in the claws of addiction and desperation. Divorce and premature death rip families apart. Families struggle with hidden problems of abuse and violence while single parents deal with the stress of "doing it all." Promiscuity persists as sexually transmitted diseases proliferate. Internet pornography sneaks its way into good homes, tearing apart husbands and wives, parents and children. Sin ricochets around our homes and communities, our churches and our nations, compromising our capacity to function as God initially intended (Plantinga, 1995).

Human functioning and the creation in which we function are remarkably ingenious but terribly broken; this is the world in which Christian counselors are called to minister to the needs of others. On the positive side of the ledger, we see that people are capable of making great strides forward in life—changing, learning, growing, adapting. On the negative side, we see that all human functioning is contaminated—our reasoning and passions have a prideful tilt. Flowers and weeds grow side by side.

Functional Problems Bring People to Counselors

The weeds of life—the functional problems that visit individuals, couples and families—bring people to counselors. One of our primary responsibilities as counselors is to help people function better.

Tyrone has been struggling with sadness and lethargy since his wife passed away three years ago. On the insistence of his children, he agrees to schedule an appointment with a counselor. Tyrone and his children both recognize that something is wrong; he seeks a more hopeful, productive and joyous life than what he currently experiences.

Julie comes for help because her impatience keeps her from being the parent she wants to be. She finds herself stressed and irritated with her children, yelling sometimes rather than talking calmly, and she wants to do better.

Jeannette freezes in front of people, but her recent job promotion requires her to give public talks at least once a month. She looks for a counselor to help her function better in speaking situations.

Like Tyrone, Julie and Jeannette, many come to counselors with functional problems as one might go to a tire store to have a flat repaired. Something is wrong, and they need to get it working again; they want to be patched up and put back on the road. We sometimes fail to see the importance and simple goodness of the counseling-as-tire-store request, and so we fail to offer practical help. The client says, "Help me get fixed up so I can function again." One counselor responds, "Tell me about your earliest childhood memory." Another counselor queries, "How is your spiritual health?" Though it may be true that the client's functional deficits are related to earlier relationships or spiritual factors, the pressing and immediate need is to address what is going wrong today. And rather than thinking of this as a naive or superficial request from our clients, we counselors ought to remember that effective functioning is a good thing. We were created to func-

---

COUNSELING TIP 6.1: *Functional First*

One of the best ways to build rapport with clients is to focus on their functional problems first, before delving into the structural and relational issues described in chapters seven and eight. Most people do not seek counseling in order to better understand their childhood experiences or their false beliefs. Rather, they come because they are functioning poorly and want to do better. By joining with the client toward a common set of functional goals, the counselor becomes a trustworthy and hope-inspiring companion on the healing journey.

---

tion well, making it appropriate for our clients to seek help in the matters of daily living and for us to provide it as we are able.

The functional domain of Integrative Psychotherapy (McMinn & Campbell, 2007) is symptom-based, helping clients identify and address the particular thoughts, feelings and behaviors that are causing them trouble (see figure 6.1). It is problem-focused and time-limited, sharing much in common with behavioral and cognitive therapies of psychology and the mercy ministries of pastoral counseling. Methods of psychology and pastoral counseling can be quite useful in helping people function better. For example, cognitive therapy helps people appraise life situations in ways that are less upsetting to them, and as a result they feel and function better. Ample scientific evidence supports the efficacy of cognitive therapy (Butler, Chapman,

Forman & Beck, 2006). Similarly, a range of behavioral methods and interpersonal therapy methods are highly effective in helping people function better. These methods are part of God's common grace, offered to every person regardless of faith beliefs.

As important as functional domain interventions are, they are often not

---

IN THE OFFICE 6.1: Helping Jeannette

Standard cognitive and behavioral techniques may be quite useful in helping Jeannette become more comfortable in public-speaking situations. Behavioral strategies could include relaxation training, breathing training, role-playing and rehearsing talks in contexts similar to the actual speaking situation. Cognitive strategies help her refocus her runaway thoughts.

Mark: Now as you were speaking on Thursday and feeling the terror and panic you're describing, what were you saying to yourself?

Jeannette: I was just thinking about how terrible the talk was going. I was feeling flushed, so I knew I was getting those red splotchy spots on my neck. And someone got up to leave, so I know I was being boring.

Mark: Okay, so let's take a moment and look at these thoughts. You mentioned that the person left because you were boring.

Jeannette: Well, that's what I assume.

Mark: Are there other possible explanations for why someone would leave?

Jeannette: Yes, I mean she could have needed to use the restroom, or maybe she had a phone call or something.

Mark: But at the moment it seemed clear it was because you were boring her?

Jeannette: [chuckles] Yeah, it seemed pretty clear.

Mark: So if you were back in the same situation now, what would be a more reasonable way to talk to yourself?

This basic thought-restructuring approach could also be used with Jeannette's fears of having red splotches on her neck. She may not have had them at all, and even if she did, it would not have been as catastrophic as she was assuming.

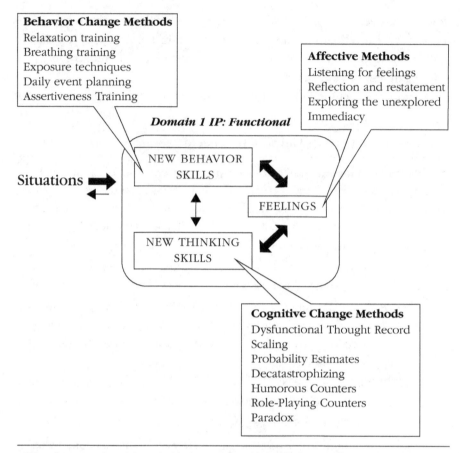

Figure 6.1. Functional domain interventions involve helping clients learn new behavioral and cognitive skills (adapted from McMinn & Campbell, 2007).

enough. Many clients need to venture into the structural and relational domains before their counseling work is complete. These other domains are explored in chapters seven and eight.

I have just offered a rationale for functionally based therapies that goes something like this:

1. Creation is good, and humans' capacity to function is stunning;

2. Still, in our fallen world, sin has tainted both creation and human functioning;

3. As a result, people come to our counseling offices wanting to function better, and it is good for counselors to help them.

This is a reasonable argument based on broad assumptions of a Christian worldview. As such, it will be deemed acceptable by almost any Christian who cares to read a book such as this. Integrationists have generally been content with this macro perspective; it provides rationale for the services we offer without requiring us to think very much about matters of individual sin in our counseling work. In contrast, biblical counselors and ministers have tried to move beyond this macro view toward a micro view that probes the problem of sin in individuals' lives (Monroe, 2001).

Sin Is Active and Personal

Sin is a ubiquitous state of brokenness that affects every aspect of creation, including every human being, but if we only see sin as generic and nonspecific then we have failed to understand the active strength of sin at work in our personal lives. The apostle Paul describes sin as a personal, aggressive, pernicious, even predatory, force in his life:

> So the trouble is not with the law, for it is spiritual and good. The trouble is with me, for I am all too human, a slave to sin. I don't really understand myself, for I want to do what is right, but I don't do it. Instead, I do what I hate. But if I know that what I am doing is wrong, this shows that I agree that the law is good. So I am not the one doing wrong; it is sin living in me that does it.
>
> And I know that nothing good lives in me, that is, in my sinful nature I want to do what is right, but I can't. I want to do what is good, but I don't. I don't want to do what is wrong, but I do it anyway. But if I do what I don't want to do, I am not really the one doing wrong; it is sin living in me that does it.
>
> I have discovered this principle of life—that when I want to do what is right, I inevitably do what is wrong. I love God's law with all my heart. But there is another power within me that is at war with my mind. This power makes me a slave to the sin that is still within me. Oh, what a miserable person I am! Who will free me from this life that is dominated by sin and death? Thank God! The answer is in Jesus Christ our Lord. So you see how it is: In my mind I really want to obey God's law, but because of my sinful nature I am a slave to sin. (Rom 7:14-25)

Functional approaches to counseling, informed by cognitive and behavioral theories in psychology, can easily overlook a Christian view of personal sin. This is not merely a problem for nonreligious therapists—even Christian counselors may slip into a complacent acceptance of the prevailing systems of cognitive and behavioral psychology. As a result, we may assume that functional problems are due to faulty learning patterns and skills deficits, and that effective counseling involves helping people learn new perspec-

---

SURVEY SAYS 6.1: Sin and Human Functioning

Several Christian leaders responding to our survey emphasized the functional nature of sin—how it trips us up and causes us problems in our daily living.

> I would like to see the field of psychology place more emphasis on human responsibility for the choices that bring about difficult consequences for people's lives.
>
> Sin is real and is very much instrumental in the problems we face each day. The problem with guilt is not lack of education—it is the need for repentance.
>
> Sin is a reality and must be admitted, repented of and forgiven by God! It is not enough to blame our sin on upbringing, tragic events or circumstances.
>
> Sin is rebellion, not just brokenness.

Sin is not merely a generic state of brokenness or a theological concept, but it is an aggressive force that every Christian battles against—or ought to. And it has implications for our psychological functioning (though the relationship between sin and psychological functioning is often complex; see Survey Says 5.1).

---

tives and skills in order to function better. This is partly right, of course, but it fails to plumb the depths of human character (see Jones & Butman, 1991, for a helpful analysis).

Tyrone—introduced earlier in this chapter—is depressed and struggling to function since his wife's death. He has turned to Internet pornography to soothe his loneliness. His depression is caused by the macro problems of a fallen world, as evidenced by his wife's premature death and the loneliness that settles on a human being living east of Eden. His counselor needs to understand a large view of sin—Tyrone struggles under the burden of brokenness that affects every person. But Tyrone's struggles are also complicated by the false movements of his heart—turning to pornography to help deal with his pain and grief rather than to spiritual companions in the context of Christian community. He needs a counselor who will understand both a macro and a micro view of sin and grace.

Julie is impatient with her children. She appreciates a counselor who listens well, empathizes with the stress she experiences and helps her function better. After all, her problem reflects a general state of broken-ness in the world, and the new cognitive and behavioral strategies she learns will help her do better. But she also needs someone to whom she can confess her yelling as sinful, who will allow her to repent and ac-knowledge that hurting her children with words is a terrible thing that of-fends God while simultaneously wounding other human beings. And she needs the sort of grace that reflects God's care and acceptance despite her sin. Julie may also need to move toward a greater awareness of her mo-tives, expectations, habits and assumptions that are derived from her fam-ily of origin, which would lead her into structural and relational domains of intervention.

Jeannette has a social phobia, which can be treated quickly and effec-tively. She did not choose her phobia—it is some combination of genetics, social demands, personality style and environmental cues that causes her to panic in front of a group. But in the process of treatment, it is possible that Jeannette will confront the sort of idolatry that we all find so pernicious and persistent—the idolatry of impression management. We care so much about what others think of us that the desire for approval ferments into self-focused obsession. It seems harsh to label this sin, though it certainly reflects something of a sinful human disposition.

The human heart is twisted and distorted, not only in a passive sense that affirms a generic state of brokenness in the world but also in an ac-tive, personal sense. Each of us is a sinner in need of grace, and we face functional consequences of our sin and the sins committed against us. Christian counselors do well to consider both a macro and micro perspec-tive of sin, and then to respond in ways that affirm God's lavish grace re-vealed in Jesus Christ. Christian psychologists involved in integration have focused on the macro view of human brokenness, and rightly so. But in our efforts to extend grace to our clients, we may have veered too far away from considering personal patterns of sin. As a result, we confuse grace with being nice.

But exploring personal sin requires great caution in counseling because human souls are vulnerable and easily wounded, especially souls that are distressed and struggling. If sin is confronted without grace, or if the coun-selor probes too directly before adequate rapport is established, one of God's precious children may be hurt rather than helped in the counseling process.

Our Words for Sin Affect Our Views of Grace

Barbara Brown Taylor (2000), an Episcopal priest, argues compellingly that we have exchanged a Christian language of sin for two alternative vocabularies. One alternative is a medical vocabulary in which people are viewed as sick rather than sinful. If we are sick, then we need treatment. Clearly there is value to this vocabulary, and people often need treatment for sickness. But if we reduce all human problems down to sickness, then we miss the riches of confession, grace and redemption. Taylor suggests this is the error of Christian liberalism. A second alternative is the language of the legal system. In this vocabulary we are guilty of crimes and in need of punishment. Again, there is value in this vocabulary. Some people commit crimes, and sometimes punishment is right. But if the human problem is reduced to crime, we again miss the riches of grace and redemption, and we reduce God to a list-keeper who cares about behavioral compliance more than relationship. Such a view of sin points fingers, elevates one sinner above another, and ultimately destroys the power of the Christian message and the appeal of Christian community. Taylor suggests this is the error of Christian fundamentalism.

Taylor's analysis can be transferred to the world of Christian counseling. Some counselors seem content with the diagnostic systems of the mental health establishment. They see functional problems as the result of past reinforcement patterns and faulty self-talk. They speak the psychological language of sickness and treatment rather than a theological language of sin and grace. Other counselors can be so focused on personal transgressions that they base their counseling methods on direct confrontation and rooting out sin from their clients' lives. These counselors seem convinced that psychological problems are God's punishment for sinful behavior, much as a criminal is punished for breaking the law. Consider how Tyrone, Julie and Jeannette might be viewed from each of these vantage points:

	Tyrone	Julie	Jeannette
Counselor A (sickness orientation)	Tyrone has a complicated grief reaction. His pornography use is understandable given his condition.	Julie is simply repeating the behavior she experienced in her childhood home. She needs to learn new patterns of behavior.	Jeannette has a social phobia. She needs to learn effective self-talk and how to interpret social cues differently.

	Tyrone	Julie	Jeannette
Counselor B (crime orientation)	Tyrone is not recovering from his grief because he has chosen a sinful and idolatrous way of coping.	Julie has hardened her heart toward her own parents, choosing to be resentful rather than forgiving. As a result, she is repeating their bad patterns.	Jeannette has become too self-focused. Her prideful focus on how she appears to others causes her to feel anxious and afraid.

One sort of counselor overlooks sin, the other overlooks transforming grace; both have mistaken and misrepresented the Christian doctrines of sin and grace.

Some people are sick, and some are criminals, but we all are sinners longing for grace. God, whose purpose is to redeem broken relationships—even at enormous cost—is justifying, sanctifying and someday glorifying us for the eternal joy of shalom. By acknowledging both sin and grace, we choose the path of Christian spirituality and introduce the hope of turning from our prideful ways, of confessing how we have hurt God, others and ourselves, and of seeking the growth and hope that comes with restored relationship. Counselor C retains a Christian view of sin and grace.

	Tyrone	Julie	Jeannette
Counselor C (sin-and-grace orientation)	Tyrone is a hurting soul, longing for connection. Sadly, he has turned in the wrong direction to receive the love and affection he needs.	Julie is struggling to parent in godly ways, partly because she has so few models of good parenting. She needs patience, instruction and encouragement.	Jeannette is seized with self-focused fear when in a group. She needs God's grace to know that she is valuable regardless of how she performs.

I was trained as Counselor A, heavily steeped in views that reduce all human dysfunction to sickness. Early in my career I met with a man for six months to help him with his depression. We evaluated his self-talk and made some systematic adjustments to the way he looked at himself and others, and ultimately he started feeling much better. Several months after he finished treatment, I learned that he had sexually abused his niece for several years when she was a child. I pondered my therapeutic intervention, and though it may have been of some use to him, I think that I missed something much more important. I suspect he came to my office longing for a place where he could confess and enter the long spiritual process of repentance and restitution; perhaps he even hoped for forgiveness from his niece and reconciliation. This man yearned for the kind of authentic connection with a therapist that emulates a sinner's cry for God: "Give me the courage and freedom to appear naked and vulnerable in the light of your presence, confident in your unfathomable mercy" (Nouwen, 1981, p. 49). What he got instead was altered self-talk. One could argue that this is just an example of bad therapy, and it may be, but it was what I had been trained to offer. The therapeutic systems that I learned in graduate school and in my postdoctoral training do not use a language of personal sin and therefore do not provide opportunities for confession, brokenness, redemption and grace.

Sometimes I wonder about this man's niece. What sort of scars does she live with every day because of his sinful choices? I imagine what a beautiful gift it might have been for her to have her uncle speak words of repentance: "I don't know if you can ever forgive me for what I did, and I realize my sin makes it unreasonable to have any sort of continued relationship, but you need to know how terribly sorry I am for how I hurt you." The language of sin would have cleansed this man deeply and would have freed his niece also. How sad that we missed such an opportunity for healing. When we fail to allow our clients the language of sin, we risk providing symptom relief while robbing them of the chance to turn around and take the first step on a journey of repentance and change. We say we offer grace in Christian counseling, but if we do not allow a language of sin we unwittingly sabotage a Christian understanding of grace.

People come to counselors with their wounds and struggles. The counselor cares and listens and accepts, helping clients bear their unbearable burdens. If counseling is to be a place of grace, then it is not a place for harsh accusation, condemnation or preaching. But neither is it a place for excusing or ignoring sin. If we fail to let clients explore the darkest, most shameful secrets of life—or if we explain them away as only byproducts of developmental crises or poor learning patterns or difficult relationships—then we exchange the possibility of grace for simply being nice. Good counseling, like good theology, calls us to look honestly at the twisted priorities of the human heart and then to rest in the unfathomable blessing of God's grace.

COUNSELING TIP 6.2: *Creating an Environment for Confession*

In my example of working with a depressed man who had abused his niece years before, one might question how I could have done anything differently. After all, if a client does not choose to talk about his past transgressions, there is nothing a counselor can do to make him talk.

Still, I think I could have provided an environment conducive to self-exploration and confession. In the years since I saw this client, I have learned to value silence more in counseling. Sometimes in the still of a quiet moment, in the presence of grace and with the prompting of the Holy Spirit, a client chooses to venture into the terrifying domain of words that have never been spoken. Or perhaps I could have probed gently about regrets of the past, offering him opportunity to confess.

Our Hearts Function Poorly at Times

As an integrationist, I have often bristled at the biblical counselors' insistence that many functional problems are the result of "idols of the heart." This seems to oversimplify the biological, psychological, interpersonal and cultural complexities of human behavior. But still, they may have a point worth considering.

We naturally hide our personal transgressions by comparing our relatively good behavior with the "big" sins of others—embezzling, murder, oppression, abuse and so on. This externalizes sin, making it someone else's problem. But if we trace back the roots of the "big" sins, we find they begin in a place familiar to each of us: in the dark shadows of the human heart. Jesus taught, "From the heart come evil thoughts, murder, adultery, all sexual immorality, theft, lying, and slander. These are what defile you" (Mt 15:19-20). Jesus was not a cardiologist; he was not referring to throbbing atria or pulmonary arteries. The heart has always been a metaphor for the affections of the inner life. Jesus knew the human heart well. He knew it is a place where purity, love, faith and hope can be found (see Mt 5:8, 22:37; Mk 11:23; and Lk 24:32). Jesus also knew that the heart is dangerous, that it can be hard, and that it can spawn greed and adultery (Mt 13:15; 6:21; and 5:28). Our hearts are complex, made to mirror God's image, and yet that mirror is marred with sin.

Our hearts draw us to the heights of humanity, to places of joy, faith, goodness, hope, compassion and mercy. When our hearts are aligned well, the great commandments become palpable: love God with singular devotion and love our neighbor as we love ourselves (Mt 22:37-40). But in our sinful state, our passions are disordered. We fail to love well because our hearts are misaligned. Loving God becomes religious rhetoric, and loving another as oneself becomes an excuse for building self-esteem. We turn it upside down, as Alvin Plantinga (2000) notes: "Instead of loving God above all and my neighbor as myself, I am inclined to love myself above all and, indeed, to hate God and my neighbor" (p. 208). In other words, our hearts are idolatrous and filled with pride.

Our human problem with pride is well-established in the Christian tradition; for centuries pride has been considered chief among the deadly sins— the sin from which other evils emerge. John Cassian warned against pride early in the fifth century, around the same time Augustine described pride as the beginning of sin. Pope Gregory the Great informed the church of the dangers of pride in the late sixth century, and Thomas Aquinas systematized a discussion of pride in the thirteenth century. In the nineteenth century Dutch theologian Andrew Murray described pride as the root of all evil. More recently Christian apologist Harry Blamires (1963) has suggested that "in the Christian moral system the key sin is pride—that perversion of the will by which the self is asserted as the centre of the universe" (p. 89). Commenting on pride, C. S. Lewis (1952) wrote:

> According to Christian teachers, the essential vice, the utmost evil, is Pride. Unchastity, anger, greed, drunkenness, and all that, are mere fleabites in comparison: it was through Pride that the devil became the devil: Pride leads to every other vice: it is the complete anti-God state of mind.
>
> Does this seem to you to be exaggerated? If so, think it over. I pointed out a moment ago that the more pride one had, the more one disliked pride in others. In fact, if you want to find out how proud you are the easiest way is to ask yourself, "How much do I dislike it when other people snub me, or refuse to take any notice of me, or shove their oar in, or patronize me, or show off?" The point is that each person's pride is in competition with every one else's pride. It is because I want to be the big noise at the party that I am so annoyed at someone else being the big noise. (p. 109)

Social science research sheds light on the nature of human pride. We think we are better than we really are, we see our faults in faint black and white rather than in vivid color, and we assume the worst in others while assuming the best in ourselves. In other words, our hearts are idolatrous because we tend to put ourselves in front of God and neighbor.

Inflated self-assessments. The essence of pride is that we place ourselves above others. Most of us see ourselves as smarter than we really are. We also claim to be better leaders, better workers, better parents and spouses, better friends, and better money managers. Who wants to be average? So we convince ourselves we are above average.

By definition most people are average on most traits. On almost any trait, such as intelligence or anxiety or affability, most people cluster around the middle of a bell-shaped distribution. In fact, 68 percent of the population falls within the average range. With intelligence tests, for example, 68 percent of the population scores between 85 and 115. An additional 16 percent is above average, and 16 percent is below average.

If we perceived ourselves accurately, then when asked how intelligent we are, 68 percent of us would put ourselves somewhere in the average range, 16 percent above average, 16 percent below average, and so on. But that is not what happens when people are asked how intelligent they are. Most people—almost everyone—will say they are at least average. Many more than 16 percent will say they are above average. And this is not only true for intelligence but also for almost any positive trait measured.

Moroney (2000) offers several fascinating examples of inflated self-assessments. For example, when the Educational Testing Service asked nearly one million high school students how well they got along with their peers, all of them rated themselves as average or above; of those, 60 percent believed themselves to be in the top 10 percent, and 25 percent believed themselves to be in the top 1 percent! What about college professors? Certainly these educated elite would have accurate perceptions of their abilities, right? When college professors were asked to rate the quality of their teaching, they were not any more realistic than the high school students. Two percent reported they were below average, 10 percent saw themselves as average, 63 percent described themselves as above average, and 25 percent said they were truly exceptional. This, of course, is statistically impossible. None of us wants to be average or below, so we simply fix the problem by perceiving ourselves to be above average.

Our prideful tendency toward self-serving comparison has clinical implications for human functioning. In the midst of an argument with a loved

> ## COUNSELING TIP 6.3: *How Do Others See You in That Regard?*
>
> Inflated self-assessments are common, even in clients who have signifi-cant self-image problems. Counselors cannot be very forceful, though, be-cause it may further damage a client's self-image or cause defensiveness in the counseling relationship. The following sorts of statements would *not* be advisable:
>
> > "I don't think you're as easy to get along with as you think you are."
> >
> > "You see yourself as a really good worker, but it seems to me that wouldn't lose so many jobs if that were true."
>
> A gentler way to probe faulty self-assessments is to ask how others per-ceive the client. This gives the client opportunity to think differently with-out creating as much of an adversarial tone between counselor and client. For example:
>
> > "You mention that you're easy to get along with. How do others that know you well see you in that regard?"
> >
> > "What do you suppose your employers, past or present, would have to say about your work if they were sitting with us today?"

one, we rarely conclude, "Her opinion is better reasoned than mine." In-stead, our pride leads us to say, "I can't believe how stupid she is being. Why can't she see this the right way?" We assume our opinions and beliefs to be better than those of others. If I recall a memory different from how someone else recalls it, I assume my recollection is correct and the other person is confused.

In the New Testament the apostle Paul wrote, "As God's messenger, I give each of you this warning: Be honest in your estimate of yourselves, measur-ing your value by how much faith God has given you" (Rom 12:3). Most of us have excessive faith in ourselves and not enough faith in the opinions of others.

Not only do we perceive ourselves as more capable than we really are, we also perceive ourselves to be more upright and moral than most others. One polling expert put it this way: "It's the great contradiction: the average person believes he is a better person than the average person" (Berke, as cited in Epley and Dunning, 2000, p. 861). Sixteen centuries earlier Augustine (398/1986) bemoaned: "[My] sin was all the more incurable because I did not judge myself to be a sinner" (p. 80). People's overestimation of themselves is a robust finding in social science. We think we are better than others—more ethical, considerate, industrious, cooperative, fair and loyal. People think they obey the Ten Commandments more consistently than others. We do this not so much because we underestimate others but because we overestimate ourselves. Our tendency is to see others as the sinners they are and to see ourselves as the perfected saints we are not.

Long before social scientists discovered our tendency to think too highly of our spiritual virtues, religious and devotional writers were saying the same thing. Back in the eighteenth century the great American theologian Jonathan Edwards (1746/1996) warned about our prideful tendencies:

> It can be recognized when one compares himself to others when he thinks he is an eminent saint in comparison. . . . "I am holier than you" (Isaiah 65:5). In taking the high place, they are doing what Christ condemns (Luke 14:7). They are confident that they are guides to the blind, but they are the blind in actuality (Romans 2:19, 20). But he whose heart is subject to Christian humility has a very different attitude. For humility, or true lowliness of mind, causes people to think others better than themselves (Philippians 2:3). (p. 130)

Attribution errors. The pride of the human heart is also revealed in how we perceive our own successes and failures, and those of others. When something bad happens, we tend to explain it by saying it is someone else's fault. It wasn't a fair test, the person next to me was making noise, the professor teaches poorly and so on. So how do we explain good outcomes? Scores of research studies demonstrate that we tend to take personal credit when good things happen: I deserve it, I am a hard worker, I am smart, etc.

Consider the implications. When something bad happens, we blame others. When something good happens, we take credit for it. A person wins the chess game because he is smart; he loses because the other player was distracting him by humming. She gets hired because she is talented; she is not hired because another applicant is willing to compromise ethics to get ahead. If people like the sermon, it's because I am a good speaker; if people fall asleep, it's because they are obstinate. Our pride allows us to recast the story so that we look acceptable regardless of the outcome.

It gets even more complicated when looking at bad events that happen to others. When something bad happens to us, we blame others; but when something bad happens to others, we tend to explain it as being their own fault. If something bad happens to you, it's your fault. If something bad happens to me, it's still your fault. When I fail the exam, it's because it was a bad test. However, when you fail, it's because you did not study enough. When I get a speeding ticket, it's because the police officer needed to fill a quota at the end of the month. But when you get a speeding ticket, it's because you drive too fast. We blame others for their failures, and we blame them for ours too.

These attribution errors are not deliberate acts of sin; in fact, we are probably not even aware of them. But still, they demonstrate the active force of sin and how it distorts the ordered world God intended: love God first and neighbor as self. The "big" offenses we label sin are all derived from that abhorrent condition that reflects the disordered passions of our hearts: pride. We compare ourselves with others in an unrealistically favorable light. We attribute good outcomes to ourselves and bad outcomes to others. When others have misfortune, we blame them. We love ourselves more than we love others.

COUNSELING TIP 6.4: *Gentle Correction*

Attribution errors often emerge in the midst of relational conflict. It is common for counselors to witness outrageous attribution errors when working with couples in distress. At times like this, it is good to remember the wisdom of the Old Testament proverb: "A gentle answer deflects anger, / but harsh words make tempers flare. / The tongue of the wise makes knowledge appealing / but the mouth of a fool belches out foolishness" (Prov 15:1-2).

Rather than aggressively confronting an attribution error—which runs the risk of making it worse—it is better to provide gentle correction by helping the client see the situation from another vantage point. For example:

> Josh, I heard you say a minute ago that it is mostly Celeste's fault that you come home late from work, because you know that she will be critical when you arrive. I'm wondering if there are any other possible explanations for why you come home late.
>
> Celeste, a while ago you mentioned that you would never be critical if it weren't for Josh's attitude. How do you suppose that came across to Josh when you said that?

Helping clients see another perspective often allows them to gain insight into their attribution errors.

Contrasting human pride with the humility of Jesus. Berkouwer (1971) discusses the absurdity of our pride by contrasting it with the humility of Jesus. Christians hold Jesus to be divine and eternal. The New Testament author John writes of Jesus:

> In the beginning the Word already existed.
>> The Word was with God,
>> and the Word was God.
> He existed in the beginning with God.
> God created everything through him,
>> and nothing was created except through him.
> The Word gave life to everything that was created,
>> and his life brought light to everyone. (Jn 1:1-4)

And yet Jesus, who is God, humbled himself. John goes on: "So the Word became human and made his home among us. He was full of unfailing love and faithfulness" (Jn 1:14). What amazing humility! The God of the universe, the Creator of everything, became a child with flesh and blood in order to bridge the gap between God and humanity.

Given the humility of Christ, it makes sense that we who follow Christ would also be humble. The apostle Paul advises Christians in New Testament times to follow the example of Jesus:

> You must have the same attitude that Christ Jesus had.
> Though he was God,
>> he did not think of equality with God
>> as something to cling to.
> Instead, he gave up his divine privileges;
>> he took the humble position of a slave
>> and was born as a human being.
> When he appeared in human form,
>> he humbled himself in obedience to God
>> and died a criminal's death on a cross. (Phil 2:5-8)

Here we must acknowledge a puzzling contrast. Our pride—our tendency to perceive ourselves as better than we are, our inflated self-assessments—demonstrates how much we want to be like God. Meanwhile, God—the eternal and majestic Creator filled with all power, knowledge and goodness—emptied himself in the life and work of Jesus, even to the point of a violent and horrific death for trumped-up charges. Christ, the eternal Word, humbled himself. We lift ourselves up.

Hope for twisted hearts. Counselors who have tried to confront pride directly with a client recognize that it often makes things worse (see Counseling Tip 3.1). This is because people protect themselves with the armor of pride, and clients become defensive if they perceive a counselor to be attacking them. We counselors do the same when we feel threatened. Beneath the armor of pride we live as vulnerable men and women longing to be loved and known. If the world were completely safe, then it would be easy to take off our armor and come together in caring community. But the world isn't safe, and it has not been for a very long time, so we live with armor. When we dare to bare ourselves, sometimes we find love and acceptance, but sometimes we find abuse and ridicule. So we make a calculated choice, perhaps unconsciously, to protect ourselves by hiding behind pride. If our deepest longing in life is to be someone important—to make a mark, to be the perfect parent, the top of the class or the best employee—then we better keep the armor on. But what if all those goals are merely the glimmer of the armor, the distractions of disordered passions? What if the deeper yearning of the human soul is to love and be loved? Then our hope is found in cautiously shedding our armor in the safety of caring relationships, acknowledging that we are vulnerable and clinging to the possibility of grace.

Ideally, Christian counselors offer this sort of grace, helping people shed the armor of prideful self-defense by providing a safe and honest relationship—while being careful not to compromise honesty for the sake of safety or vice versa. When counselors disregard the possibility of sin, they inadvertently cheapen grace; when they disregard grace, they heighten their clients' defensiveness. Blaise Pascal, the seventeenth-century mathematician and philosopher, wrote: "Man is nothing but a subject full of natural error that cannot be eradicated except through grace" (1660/1966, p. 42). Pascal implies two possibilities. Either we can spend our time denying our natural error, or we can set aside the armor and cry out for grace. When we spend all our efforts trying to convince ourselves and others that we are better than we really are, we only end up spinning a web of self-deception. But if we accept the truth and recognize how natural error pervades every part of our existence, then we invite grace into our relationships with one another and with God.

Natural and Spiritual Explanations for Functional Problems

Christian counselors face an ideological clamor regarding the cause of functional problems, illustrated in figure 6.2. On one hand, the therapeutic culture in which we live offers various naturalistic explanations, often referred to as biopsychosocial. Biological factors—such as genetic constitution, disease states and brain functioning—influence how we experience life and function on a daily basis. Psychological factors include personality styles, past learning patterns, developmental processes and so on. Social factors involve the cultural context in which we function, including prevailing values, mores and norms.

On the other hand, biblical counselors and many pastoral care leaders emphasize the spiritual forces causing functional problems. These spiritual forces involve the general condition of sin that makes every person vulnerable to problems and the personal patterns of sin that further complicate life. The problem of pride reflects both our general state of brokenness and our specific idolatries of putting ourselves in front of God and others. In addition, Christians believe that supernatural forces are working behind the scenes. The apostle Paul puts it clearly:

> Put on all of God's armor so that you will be able to stand firm against all strategies of the devil. For we are not fighting against flesh-and-blood enemies, but against evil rulers and authorities of the unseen world, against mighty powers in this dark world, and against evil spirits in the heavenly places.
>
> Therefore, put on every piece of God's armor so you will be able to resist the enemy in the time of evil. Then after the battle you will still be standing firm. Stand your ground, putting on the belt of truth and the body armor of God's righteousness. (Eph 6:11-14)

Paul's words also suggest the importance of spiritual growth. As we grow in the knowledge and experience of God we find grace to better withstand the troubles of life in a broken world.

Sadly, Christian counselors have polarized. The integrationist movement,

Naturalistic Explanations | **Christian Counselors** | **Spiritual Explanations**

Biology — Christian Counselors — State of Brokenness
Childhood Development — Personal Sin
Personality — Supernatural Forces
Environment — Lack of Spiritual Growth

Figure 6.2. The cause of functional problems

deeply influenced by the broader psychological establishment, has leaned toward naturalistic explanations. I remember being told in graduate school that spiritual explanations for problems "went out in the Middle Ages." Not surprisingly, I emerged from graduate training with a strong preference for naturalistic explanations of functional problems. Biblical counselors have leaned toward supernatural explanations. They tend to distrust psychology, preferring instead to use special revelation as a guide for understanding human struggles and healing. Collectively, we have tended to emphasize the faults in the other perspective, reflecting our problem with pride even as we pursue truth, rather than seeing that both perspectives may have something important to offer. Just as good marital therapists seek to find value in both spouse's perspectives, so also we would be wise to seek truth in both naturalistic and spiritual explanations of psychological problems. In doing so, we honor God's order and character, revealed in both general and special revelation.

Grace-filled Christian counseling accepts the possibility of natural explanations, thereby avoiding an accusing tone that implies suffering people are experiencing the consequences of their sinful choices. Life is hard; natural explanations help counselors empathize with others regarding the difficult circumstances they face. Tyrone's depression subsequent to his wife's death is related to complex processes of attachment involving brain systems and physiological functioning, cultural understandings of grief, personality factors, and his own developmental history that set a context for understanding death and loss. Julie's irritability with her children is certainly influenced by cortisol levels related to life stress, the way she was raised by her parents, the level of social support she experiences and various other psychological factors. Jeannette's social phobia is shaped by her autonomic nervous system, dysfunctional beliefs and faulty self-talk as well as her past experiences speaking in public.

And grace-filled Christian counseling *also* accepts the reality of spiritual explanations. If we fail to acknowledge sin, then we foreclose on the possibility of confession, repentance and growth in godliness. Tyrone has turned to Internet pornography to soothe his pain. Paradoxically, it only adds to his pain and sense of isolation. A wise counselor will allow Tyrone the dignity to acknowledge and confess his sin and turn back to healthier patterns of relating to others. Julie knows that yelling at her children is intrinsically damaging and wrong toward them. She wants a counselor to understand and empathize with her difficult life circumstances, but she also needs a counselor who will help her turn from her sin so that she can become a more consistent and loving parent. Jeannette's social phobia may be primarily related to naturalistic explanations, but it will also be helpful for her to consider how intensely self-focused she becomes in speaking situations. Pride turns our eyeballs inside-out so that we have a fixed inward gaze; we obsess about ourselves rather than seeing the people and creation around us. In this sense, a social phobia is a spiritual issue as well as a psychological malady.

Sin has become a harsh word because we have divorced it from the doctrine of grace, and so Christian counselors are viewed as primitive or abusive if they associate functional problems with sinful patterns. But growth in grace requires us to recover a healthy understanding of sin—not in order to promote shame, but to emphasize the greatness and boundless love of God and the hope found in establishing an identity that is bigger than self-interest. Jonathan Edwards (1746/1996) wrote: "But the more eminent that saints are, the more they will have the light of heaven in their souls. Thus they will appear to themselves to be the more debased and sinful. They can only cover themselves with the righteousness of Christ, and allow their own deficiencies to be swallowed up and hid in the beams of His abundant glory and love" (p. 134).

7

Sin and Grace
in the Structural Domain

WE ONCE HAD A FAMILY DOG, CHALE, who was a great joy to Lisa and not as much to me. (I am an Oregon farm boy who has never understood why someone would voluntarily bring a hairy, smelly beast indoors.) As difficult as it was having an animal residing in our house, I must admit that Chale was a rich source of illustrations for writing and teaching. Lisa's opinion was that Chale was excited to be in our presence; mine was that Chale was excited about the possibility of food, which she associated with our presence. So I tested it out, as social scientists do, by observing Chale over twenty-four consecutive intervals, each lasting thirty seconds. Half the time I was holding food and half the time I was not. I discovered that Chale stood, paid attention and salivated when I had food in my hand, and she ignored me when I was foodless. I videotaped my informal scientific study, timed and averaged her standing and sitting, and converted it all to a PowerPoint lecture for my classes (see figure 7.1). Lisa and my students were never as compelled by my scientific study as I was. Perhaps my presuppositions contaminated my scientific methods at least a bit.

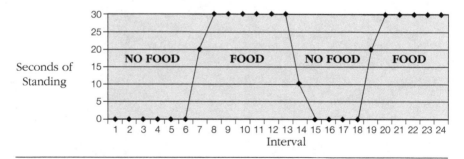

Figure 7.1. Pseudo-science with Chale

However tainted my science may have been, it reflected a natural hierarchy between Chale and me. She was the object of study—the one who stood, wagged her tail and salivated when she sensed food in my hand—and I was the one capable of collecting and interpreting the data, transferring the video to PowerPoint, and using it to explain ABAB research designs to my students. The capacity of a human person far exceeds the capacity of a dog. Humans set the rules and dogs follow—at least when the humans are around to monitor the rules! Humans go to work each day in order to pay the rent or mortgage payment while their dogs lie around, bark at the neighbors and the mail carrier, urinate on various yard ornaments, and dig holes in the backyard. People provide and prepare food for themselves and for the dog. Dogs eat and then lie around some more. Humans plan for the future, delaying gratification as needed. Dogs climb onto the counter and eat the blueberry pie that was prepared for a future human event.

My analysis is not limited to dogs; humans are set apart from all the animal kingdom. As excited as scientists get when they discover that chimpanzees are capable of symbolic communication and primitive language, the more remarkable thing is to consider the vast intellectual gap between humans and the brightest animals. We have structural capacities that far exceed other animals. Theologically speaking, this is because humans are created in the image of God and other animals are not. We have been blessed with an ontological essence that bears resemblance to the nature of God.

> O LORD, our Lord, your majestic name fills the earth!
>> Your glory is higher than the heavens.
> You have taught children and infants
>> to tell of your strength,
> silencing your enemies
>> and all who oppose you.
>
> When I look at the night sky and see the work of your fingers—
>> the moon and the stars you set in place—
> what are mere mortals that you should think about them,
>> human beings that you should care for them?
> Yet you made them only a little lower than God,
>> crowned them with glory and honor.
> You gave them charge of everything you made,
>> putting all things under their authority—
> the flocks and the herds,
>> and all the wild animals,

COUNSELING TIP 7.1: *Balancing Cognitive Challenges with Acceptance*

The methods of cognitive therapy are powerful and effective. However, these methods almost always involve some degree of challenging a client's thoughts, so they need to be tempered with good therapeutic rapport and sensitivity to the counseling relationship. Think of challenging a client's thoughts and accepting the client as two sides on a balance. Cognitive change techniques involve challenging, which is fine, but too much challenge tips the scales and makes the relationship seem unsafe. Conversely, acceptance is an essential part of effective counseling, but if the Christian counselor offers nothing more than acceptance the client may miss important opportunities for growth and insight.

---

the birds in the sky, the fish in the sea,
   and everything that swims the ocean currents.

O LORD, our Lord, your majestic name fills the earth! (Ps 8)

The psalmist's response is proper; our human structural capacities should cause our jaws to drop in wonder of our spectacular Creator. Created in God's image, humans have the capacity to reason, use complex language forms, articulate and conform to moral standards, and so on. All the conveniences of contemporary life, ranging from printed media to wireless broadband, reflect the creative genius of God that is reflected in human ontology. Reasoning allows us to contemplate big ideas, to communicate them with one another, to test their validity and revise them accordingly. Our human capacities also allow us to engage in relationship with God in ways that dogs and chimpanzees could never imagine; we can contemplate God's majesty and grace, engage in spiritual disciplines, and restrain our impulses when immediate desires and moral principles conflict. Not surprisingly, these God-given structural capacities form the bases of some helpful approaches to counseling.

Schema-Based Counseling

The prevailing counseling paradigm taught in research-oriented graduate programs is cognitive therapy. Cognitive therapy capitalizes on human ontology by helping people use their reasoning abilities to alter how they are thinking about themselves, others and life situations. Rather than being captured in fear when standing in front of a group of people, a person can learn to reappraise the situation, use calming self-talk and feel better. Similarly, a depressed person can learn to reevaluate the thoughts that are causing dismal feelings. People in a troubled relationship can learn to think differently about their partner, which often helps the relationship improve.

Cognitive therapists speak of various levels of thoughts. On the surface, above the threshold of consciousness are automatic thoughts. Clifford, a depressed man, may wake in the morning and say, "This is going to be a terrible day. I hate my job, I hate my coworkers, I hate my life." These automatic thoughts are accessible and relatively easy to change with some basic cognitive therapy techniques. Beneath automatic thoughts are more general cognitions known as intermediate beliefs. They are less accessible to consciousness and are not contingent on specific situations. Clifford may have

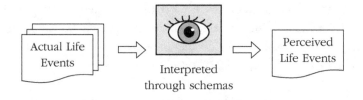

Figure 7.2. Schemas shape our perceptions of the world

an intermediate belief, "I am bound to fail and disappoint people." This predisposes him to dread going to work. The deepest level of beliefs—core beliefs—are the most general and least accessible to consciousness. Perhaps Clifford believes he is fundamentally vile and unlovable. Core beliefs are generally established early in life, often in the context of formative relationships, and they are associated with a complex array of other thoughts, emotions, motivations, behaviors and physiological responses. These "packets" of experience are known as schemas. Schemas serve as roadmaps to help a person navigate the complexity of life (see figure 7.2). But, like roadmaps, schemas are sometimes mistaken, leading people to false and damaging conclusions about themselves, others and the nature of the world. These false and damaging schemas can be disarmed in the process of counseling as clients learn to distance themselves from old ways of thinking and learn new ways to view the world.

Schema-based therapies are gaining a good deal of attention in counseling (e.g., Young, Klosko & Weishaar, 2003). This reflects the general growth of cognitive science in psychology (Robins, Gosling & Craik, 1999) as well as increasing clinical research evidence demonstrating the effectiveness of cognitive therapy (Butler, Chapman, Forman & Beck, 2006).

In Integrative Psychotherapy (McMinn & Campbell, 2007), the second domain of treatment is structural (see figure 7.3). In this domain we evaluate and reconsider the schemas through which clients interpret the events in their lives. For instance, a person who believes "God loves me and wants to be in relationship with me" will have a vastly different experience in life than the one who believes "God is profoundly angry and disappointed with me." Maladaptive schemas are somewhat malleable, which means that counselors can help clients to reevaluate the beliefs and assumptions that are causing them trouble.

Integrative Psychotherapy involves a process called Recursive Schema Activation, which allows a person to develop a new identity apart from the old dysfunctional schemas. The process of Recursive Schema Activation bears resemblance to the apostle Paul's distinction between the "old self" and the "new self" (see Rom 6:6; Eph 4:22-24; Col 3:9-11; also see Roberts, 2001).

A Christian Appraisal of Schema-Based Therapies

Christian counselors are wise to have a mixed reaction to the popularity of schema-based cognitive therapy. On one hand, these therapies reflect the stunning beauty of human ontology. Our capacity to reason is so robust that we can learn to control our propensity to depression or anxiety or any number of other maladies. On the other hand, in the process of helping people move from misaligned thinking to greater alignment, cognitive therapists draw on assumptions that do not always fit well with a Christian worldview.

Schema-based therapies are based on the assumption that people develop faulty, self-deprecating assumptions that cause emotional disturbances. These maladaptive schemas come from childhood experiences and relationships. Virtually any experienced counselor or pastor is likely to agree with this premise; they have all seen the tragic effects of abusive and difficult childhood events. People who have been scarred by formative relationships often are prone to shame, difficulty forming healthy relationships and various other self-defeating patterns. And almost any counselor will agree that people improve as they are able to change their thinking. If a depressed

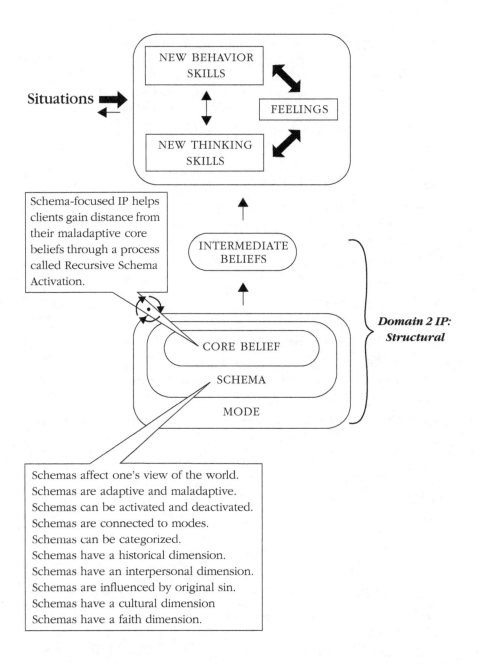

Figure 7.3. Structural domain interventions involve working with schemas (adapted from McMinn & Campbell, 2007).

IN THE OFFICE 7.1: Recursive Schema Activation

Recursive Schema Activation is a core strategy of Integrative Psychotherapy. The idea is to activate a client's schema by focusing on an emotion-laden experience in everyday life and then help the person gain some psychological and emotional distance from the schema. This is done over and over until a person begins to develop a new identity apart from the old way of seeing the world.

Mark: That sounds like a challenging evening with your husband.

Kendra: Yeah, I mean we had agreed several days earlier that we were going out on a date, but he should know that I don't like Cuban food. I can't believe he made the reservations without even asking me.

Mark: What were your emotions when he told you that's where you were going for dinner?

Kendra: I felt really angry!

Mark: What else?

Kendra: I don't know. Maybe just like he doesn't care that much or something, like he doesn't value my opinion.

Mark: Right. Sort of like what we talked about last week. If people value me, they will provide for my needs.

Kendra: I guess it is similar. It pushed an old button, like how I felt when my parents would just pick up and move without even consulting my sister and me.

Mark: So that same script was playing Friday night.

Kendra: Yes, I suppose so.

[Silence]

Kendra: I know it's not that way with Mike. He cares about me. He told me later he just forgot that I don't like Cuban food and that he was trying to surprise me with something different.

Mark: What do you think about that now?

Kendra: He's a sweet man. I wish I would have responded differently on Friday.

Mark: But it makes some sense why you didn't.

Kendra: Yes, thank you. I know that's right. I feel like I'm learning all these new things about myself.

client can stop thinking of herself as a loser, and instead realize that she is deeply valued by God and others, then she will naturally become less depressed. Similarly, an angry man might believe the world is a competitive battlefield; if he can realign his assumptions, then he will be less angry and demanding. These basic assumptions of cognitive therapy can be shared among counselors regardless of their faith beliefs.

But from a Christian counseling vantage point, the problem is worse than cognitive therapists typically acknowledge. Cognitive therapists typically assume the neutrality of human nature. They assume the same sort of blank slate (tabula rasa) that their predecessors—the behavior therapists—advocated. The child is born neutral, and then both good and bad thinking patterns are developed in relation to interactions with others. As a result, all distorted schemas and misaligned thinking are deemed to come from unfortunate prior experiences. If sin is considered at all, it is the misdeeds of parents and other caregivers whose malevolence caused the client to develop distorted views of the world.

A Christian worldview requires another layer of complexity. Christians can agree with the fundamental premises of schema-based therapy—that painful life experiences lead to distorted thinking and that realigning faulty thinking produces good changes in mood and behavior. We can also agree that painful early life experiences can have negative consequences for how one views the world. But cognitive therapists understate the problem when they assume a neutral beginning of life. A Christian worldview calls us to embed our views of misaligned thinking in a broader context of original and personal sin that lends itself to the pernicious problem of egoism. Even the person coming from an excellent home is prone to distorted thinking—not only because of parents or early peer relations but because sin is an active force that twists our proper priorities and elevates love of self far above the love of God and neighbor. This means that distorted thinking can appear as being both self-deprecating and negative or it can also be self-inflating and overly flattering. In either case, one's focus is on the self, rather than God or neighbor. Some therapists may contribute unwittingly to a client's egoism problem at the same time as relieving the client of self-deprecating assumptions.

Kendra sees a Christian counselor because of her struggles with body image and poor self-esteem. After years of struggling with various eating disorders and chronic anxiety, she has decided it is time to seek help. The first job of the counselor is to listen well to Kendra's story. Born in the tumultuous 1960s, Kendra recalls her parents as good-hearted people whose lives were too chaotic to provide a stable home environment. Some of her childhood years were spent living in a commune; others were spent moving from town to town as her parents drifted from one job to another. By the time her parents "found themselves" and settled into stable careers, Kendra was a junior high school student trying to bring some sense of control to her unpredictable world. She found that food brought a measure of control—both to her own life, because nobody else could tell her what to eat, and in how others related to her. As the counselor listens to her story, a prominent schema becomes clear: "I must stay in control or else my life will decompensate into chaos." This schema predisposes Kendra to anxiety because she is unable to attain the sort of control she believes is necessary. Life is unpredictable and a bit messy, which is troubling for a woman who has spent her life trying to get away from the messiness of life.

This seems straightforward from a schema-therapy perspective. Kendra reacted to her early life by forming a life rule about control. This rule has helped her in certain ways, but it has also troubled and harmed her. In counseling, Kendra needs to gain greater insight about how her past connects with her present, and she needs to find ways to distance herself from her maladaptive schema. But a Christian counselor sees additional complexity in Kendra's situation. It is not just that Kendra is responding to her chaotic childhood; she also has the same egoistic, me-first propensities that every person has. Her love of control is not *only* a reaction to childhood; it is also a reflection of the sin nature that characterizes each of our lives. We so naturally enlarge our views of self and diminish our views of God and neighbor. Kendra faces a fundamental spiritual problem as well as a psychological problem. And if counseling methods offer Kendra relief from her childhood schema, it will not *only* be because of the psychological understanding that the counselor offers, but also because the therapy relationship helps Kendra understand a greater grace than she has known before. Releasing her desire for control is virtually impossible in the context of a dangerous or unpredictable relationship, but it may be possible if Kendra can find a safe, caring, gracious counselor who will speak truth while helping her explore the contours of living in a fallen and complex world. Working with Kendra is not simply a matter of changing her maladaptive schema; it also involves understanding and exploring sin in a context of grace.

COUNSELING TIP 7.2: *Accessing Schemas Through Emotion-Focused Reflection*

Helping clients identify schemas and related emotions is a natural way to confront their faulty thinking without it feeling adversarial. For example, Kendra's counselor might listen to her story and then offer an emotion-focused reflection:

> Kendra, as I listen to your story, I hear quite a lot of fear about losing control of yourself and your life situation. It seems like a theme that weaves its way through your life.

Kendra is likely to respond well to such a reflection, and it will cause her to think about the control schemas that need to be further explored in counseling. Contrast this with a more adversarial, direct approach:

> Kendra, it seems to me that you have developed a problem with control. When things don't go as you plan, you start to feel desperate and make decisions that aren't very good.

This adversarial approach is likely to evoke defensiveness, shame and anger in Kendra.

Egoism Distorts Thinking

For centuries philosophers and theologians have discussed the marvel of human rationality. Medieval theologians went so far as to suggest that human reason remains relatively trustworthy despite the damage that sin has done to moral will. That is, though we lost our moral bearings at the Tree of the Knowledge of Good and Evil, at least we retained our rational capacities. The Reformers disagreed, insisting that both our will and our rationality are profoundly compromised by sin, but following the Reformation, the Western Enlightenment brought with it an irresistible surge of optimism about human rationality. Descartes' pronouncement, *Cogito, ergo sum* ("I think, therefore I am"), elevated subjective reason even above objective truth. Much of contemporary life, including schema-based therapy, is influenced by this Enlightenment optimism about human reason. If we get stymied in life, we are told to stop and think for a while—or to go see a therapist who will help us think better—presumably because human rationality is quite trustworthy and wise. People who feel bad are told to stop their unhealthy thinking and to think differently in order to feel better.

Christians can be optimistic about many things but not about self-sufficient reasoning. We have always had limits in our ability to think, even before sin entered the picture, because we are finite. But now we are both finite and fallen. The creation story suggests Adam and Eve fell into sin because they, as finite beings, wanted to know more than they were created to know. They wanted to be like God. The serpent's lie—that eating the fruit would allow humans to know as much as God—had the opposite effect. Searching for infinite knowledge, humans went from being clear but finite thinkers to being foggy, finite thinkers. In the words of systematic theologian G. C. Berkouwer (1971), "What actually happened is that by transgressing God's commandment the eyes of man were closed" (p. 154).

Our intellect is dulled—our eyes closed—as a result of our fallen state (Moroney, 2000). In the narrow sense, the noetic effects of sin (see Counseling Tip 3.1) are that we cannot reason well enough to see our need for salvation. We do not perceive God, or our need for God, correctly. In our blindness, our dulled state of thinking, we cannot see the extent of our sin. Our only hope is found in God's grace.

> God is so rich in mercy, and he loved us so much, that even though we were dead because of our sins, he gave us life when he raised Christ from the dead. (It is only by God's grace that you have been saved!) . . . God saved you by his grace when you believed. And you can't take credit for this; it is a gift from God. (Eph 2:4-5, 8)

In a broader sense, there are many noetic effects of sin. Our rationality is dulled in various ways because all creation has fallen from its initial state. In our prideful independence we fail to see how faulty our reasoning can be, and we end up with all sorts of problems. Alvin Plantinga (2000) explains that sin "carries with it a sort of *blindness,* a sort of imperceptiveness, dullness, stupidity" (p. 207).

In the previous chapter we considered how our functional capacities are hindered by pride. Called to love God first, we end up loving self first; and called to love neighbor as self, we end up competing with neighbor in order to love self more. But pride affects more than just the heart; it also afflicts our minds. Our heads are as disarrayed as our hearts, making us vulnerable to all sorts of egoistic miscalculations and blunders. Social and cognitive scientists have studied human reasoning. Their findings affirm the magnificence of human rationality, but they are also quite humbling insofar as they reveal pervasive problems with human reason. People sometimes compare

---

SURVEY SAYS 7.1: Noetic Effects of Sin

Several respondents in our survey chose to mention or allude to the noetic effects of sin when asked what they wished psychologists knew about sin. For example:

> Sin distorts and corrupts the individual's ability to realize the depth of his [or her] problem. It seeks to blame others or outside circumstance for often personal choice.
>
> It goes deeper than overt behaviors and can encompass psychological defenses, and so on. . . . The noetic effects of sin upon the whole person.

Because we are sinners, we have difficulty seeing that we are sinners. Sin is blinding and we tend to be defensive in response. Grace has a healing effect, though, because God invites us to see again, to admit our sin and to seek forgiveness and redemption.

"If we claim we have no sin, we are only fooling ourselves and not living in the truth. But if we confess our sins to him, he is faithful and just to forgive our sins and to cleanse us from all wickedness" (1 Jn 1:8-9).

---

human cognition with computers; this is both too modest a comparison, because our human capacity and creativity far exceed that of a computer, and too flattering, because we are not nearly as systematic and objective as a computer. Our human data processing is filtered through an egoistic grid that often leads to false conclusions and strained relationships. There are many ways human thinking is distorted by egoism, including overconfidence, confirmation bias and belief perseverance.

Overconfidence. We are more confident than we are correct in our thoughts. Most all of us assume our thoughts are better reasoned, wiser and more insightful than they really are. This premise built Las Vegas and Atlantic City. Gamblers assume that probabilities apply to other people, that their own hunches will work out and other people will lose their shirts. While Hollywood tells us to believe in ourselves, studies in the social sciences tell us that we already believe too much in ourselves. Psychologists call this the overconfidence phenomenon.

The pride of overconfidence wounds people and their relationships. Kendra, introduced earlier in this chapter, was once a dear friend of Andrea. Now they are separated by the vast distance of overconfidence. Convinced that

Andrea and her husband, Jorge, were being too lenient with their two young sons, Kendra confronted Andrea, citing a few pithy Scripture verses and warning her of the damage being done by "sparing the rod." Andrea erupted in anger: "How dare you tell me how to raise my children!" Things changed. They are still friends, but a pervasive tension now taints their time together. Andrea feels uncomfortable because she hates feeling judged and criticized. Kendra, deeply wounded by Andrea's harsh words, feels misunderstood. Both are overconfident. Andrea and Jorge are sure they are raising their children well, showing the sort of kindness and understanding that neither of them experienced as children. They want something better for their children. Kendra is certain that Andrea's children are bound for a rebellious adolescence and that her words of confrontation were only meant to help her friend. She has seen lenient parenting backfire time and time again, including in her own childhood. Both Kendra and Andrea are sure they are right.

We live in a state of sin, a state in which our thinking is dulled with overconfidence, people are hurt and relationships wounded as a result. Our thinking is a great gift, but when we trust it too much, we are vulnerable to foolish and costly errors.

Confirmation bias. Overconfidence is bad enough, but it is particularly troubling when coupled with confirmation bias. That is, we actively seek information that confirms what we already believe. Most of us, when we walk into a bookstore, live out the confirmation bias as we head to a section of books that tend to confirm our beliefs. The Reformed theologian walks to the religion section to find books on Calvin; the postmodern mystic walks to the New Age section; the counselor to the self-help area; the financial analyst to the economic books. Then we pick up a few books and flip through the pages. If we like what we see, we conclude, "Oh, this looks like a good book," and we consider buying it. If we disagree with the author, we simply put the book back and conclude it is not worth our money. Rather than stretching ourselves and reading different perspectives, we look for books that confirm our ideas. After a while it seems as if "all the evidence" supports our beliefs, when actually we have failed to look at all the evidence. As a result we are blind to contradictory evidence and reluctant to change our minds even when we hold false beliefs.

Kendra and Andrea surround themselves with friends who confirm their beliefs. Shortly after Andrea's confrontation with Kendra, she and Jorge joined a church parenting class led by a like-minded couple. The class is filled with caring parents who eagerly find ways to nurture expressiveness and individuality in their children. The class is a great encouragement, affirming what Andrea and Jorge already believe about effective parenting. Kendra goes to a different church where she teaches a parenting class on raising children "God's way." Each week concurring parents gather and affirm the importance of firm discipline and clear expectations. Both Andrea and Kendra surround themselves with those who will confirm what they already believe, and their friendship remains ruptured.

Belief perseverance. In addition to overconfidence and confirmation bias, we struggle with the belief-perseverance phenomenon. That is, we cling to our beliefs even in the presence of contradictory evidence. Humans are stubborn creatures. Not only do we avoid contradictory information (confirmation bias), even when it is unavoidable and right in front of our eyes, we tend to discredit it so that we can cling to our prior beliefs (belief perseverance). We seem to hold some of our ideas until "death do us part."

Political debates are a classic demonstration of belief perseverance. Politician 1 is given a question and presents a particular viewpoint. Politician 2 then discredits it with various statistics and arguments, at which point Politician 1 ignores Politician 2's arguments and holds on to the initial viewpoint. Then it is Politician 2's turn for a question, and the same thing transpires, but with roles reversed. When the debate is over, the commentators spin a story about who "won" the debate, mostly based on the politician who was most charming in resisting the other person's arguments (or perhaps based on which politician confirmed the commentators' prior beliefs). It would be death to a politician to say, "That is a very good point. I may be incorrect in some of my assumptions." Voters do not want intellectual honesty as much as charming intractability.

Sometimes Andrea and Jorge notice that their children seem to be lost, looking for structure and guidance. At times their sons seem wild and out of control, less able than other children to constrain their impulses, and quite demanding. The parents dismiss what they see with trite reassurances: "Boys will be boys." "It's just the terrible twos." They persist in their permissive parenting, convinced they are right. Sometimes Kendra notices that her grown children lack joy and brightness. She sees amazing creativity and joy in Andrea's sons. They smile, laugh, run, jump and love life. Kendra explains it away, saying, "They may seem happy now, but just wait until they are adolescents in the juvenile correction system." Convinced they are right and impervious to contrary evidence, Kendra and Andrea continue in their beliefs. Both are partly right and partly wrong, but both think they are almost entirely right. The rift lives on.

We have three strikes against us—overconfidence, confirmation bias and belief perseverance. The effects of our pride-stained, egoistic thinking hinder our capacity to think clearly and love one another well. Two people have differing viewpoints, both believe they are correct, both are overconfident in their perspectives, both can see only the evidence that confirms what they already believe, and both will persevere in their beliefs even when faced with conflicting evidence. No wonder it is difficult to resolve conflict in relationships!

We so desperately need grace-filled relationships in which we can forgive and accept one another despite our differences, but this is no easy task when we are all so prone to distorted and egoistic thinking. If we want to understand the grip of sin in our lives, we must understand the depth of our isolation and the waywardness of our thoughts. I stand with centuries of believers before me, asserting that our errant thinking can be transformed by the grace of God, but first we must know that our thinking is fallible and often wrong so that we look to a faithful community of those who will help us distinguish truth from error. The purpose of rational discourse in Christian community is to revolutionize our thoughts to better conform to the mind of God. Because we place so much confidence in our individual reasoning, we often end up alone and isolated—churning through logic problems with minds that are more illogical than we want to admit. Our thinking can draw us toward truth and toward others, or it can distance us from both if we swap the richness of community with the poverty of isolation.

Healing Within a Community of Grace

It is no coincidence that many churches have the word *grace* in their names: Grace Chapel, Grace Community Church, Grace Fellowship and so on. The church is called to be a community of grace, where the love of Christ fills the lives of those who attend and then floods into the surrounding communities. This sort of grace is not the reality for every church, of course, but it should be an aspiration for all who call themselves followers of Christ. Christ was filled with grace and truth (Jn 1:14), and so we also are called to be Christians whose grace is firmly rooted in truth.

Those of us who call ourselves integrationists need to listen carefully to biblical counselors with regard to ecclesiology. While we have been accusing biblical counselors of being Bible-thumping fundamentalists, they have been trying to tell us that a community of faith matters in the care of souls—both to keep the counselor accountable to standards of truth and to provide a supportive community for those needing help (Powlison, 2001). It is curious that such a thing be associated with fundamentalism rather than with orthodoxy and common sense.

Several years ago I had a part-time clinical practice doing psychological evaluations with adolescents and adults at the local hospital. Week after week I found myself writing reports that had a similar recommendation: "This person needs to be connected with a stronger social support system." At some point I realized that Christians have a time-honored social and spiritual support system that deserves the attention of those offering soul-care services to people in need. I began shifting my research and consulting interests toward ways that psychology and the church can work together well (McMinn, Meek, Canning & Pozzi, 2001). Over the past decade of doing this research and consulting I have discovered many beautiful examples of how psychologists and counselors can partner with the church in ministering grace and truth to individuals, families and communities (McMinn & Dominguez, 2005).

Consider three not-so-hypothetical possibilities in response to a typical

---

COUNSELING TIP 7.3: *Beyond Toxic Faith*

Many Christian counselors and psychologists have noted that churches and church leaders can be noxious or toxic to people. This is true enough—I suspect every experienced counselor has seen examples of pathological leaders who have taken advantage of parishioners. But we should tread carefully here, because the church (collectively) has done much more good than harm over the centuries. If we are too quick to discourage people from church involvement, we may be stripping away a source of hope, meaning, obedience and encouragement. Some people need to get away from toxic church situations, and they may even need to take a break from church in the aftermath of the trauma they experience, but the long term goal should be to help Christian clients find and become part of a healthy community of believers.

counseling situation. A troubled Christian person comes to a Christian counselor for help, and the counselor notices a structural problem. Perhaps the person is not being rational and reasonable, or perhaps his or her moral capacity has been eroded by years of damage and atrophy. The counselor's task is to help the client better reflect the structural capacities of one created in God's image.

Possibility 1 is for the counselor to help the client look inward for a

---

IN THE OFFICE 7.2: Watching for Functional Relativism

Cognitive therapists naturally drift toward functional relativism—where the veracity of thoughts and beliefs are determined by the psychological effects they produce. Consider the following dialogue:

Micky: She just makes me feel like a loser husband. After a while I start to believe her. Maybe she would be better off if I just got in the car and drove away.

Counselor: When you say that, it seems to be based on the thought that Alicia is right, that you are a loser husband.

Micky: Yeah, I suppose.

Counselor: Is she right? Are you a loser husband?

Micky: I don't think I am. I mean I come home after work, I work hard, I earn an income, I don't fool around on her. I may not be the best husband in the world, but I do okay.

Counselor: And when you say those things to yourself, how do you feel?

Micky: Well, I think maybe she's being too particular. Maybe it's more her problem than mine.

Counselor: Do you still want to get in a car and drive as far as you can?

Micky: No, maybe she should drive away [chuckles]. Or maybe I just need to be okay with her not being happy with me all the time.

Counselor: So if you think you're a loser husband it makes you want to drive away, and if you remind yourself that you're a fine husband, it takes away that need to escape. Which way of thinking makes most sense to you?

Micky: Well, when you put it that way, it's best to remind myself that I'm a fairly good husband.

This may be an effective intervention, but it is troubling to choose which thoughts are best based on their psychological effects. Sometimes false thoughts make people feel good and true thoughts make them feel bad. Perhaps another approach, not as vulnerable to functional relativism, would go like this:

Micky: I don't think I am. I mean I come home after work, I work hard, I earn an income, I don't fool around on her. I may not be the best husband in the world, but I do okay.

Counselor: Those things seem important to consider. It sounds like you have some standards for what a good husband is.

Micky: Yeah. I mean I think it is important to honor the promises I made on our wedding day and to honor Scripture in how I live. I may watch a lot of television, and I don't talk as much as Alicia wants me to, and I'm not very romantic and stuff, but I keep the promises I made and really try to make sacrifices to love her well.

Counselor: If I'm hearing you right, Micky, it seems like you have two sides on this ledger. On the one side you have some things you feel good about, and on the other side you have some things that Alicia would like to see changed, and maybe you would too. How does this fit with the thought of being a loser husband?

Micky: It feels that way sometimes, and I could do better, but I'm not a loser husband. I don't think Alicia would say I am either.

In this second example, the basis for evaluation is not the mood produced by various thoughts but it is the underlying values that shape how Micky sees himself as a husband. The counselor has avoided functional relativism.

greater degree of rationality and morality. The counselor might say things such as, "Listen to your heart," or "Look inside and see what you discover about your life situation," or "How is God leading you in this situation?" Much can be said in favor of this approach. There is certainly merit to insight and personal understanding, and understanding the inner life is an important part of Christian living, emphasized for centuries by Christian contemplatives and mystics (Benner, 2005; Foster 1992, 1998). As impor-

tant as it is to look inward and to be sensitive to the guidance of the Holy
Spirit, looking inward for truth needs to be balanced with other means of
discovery. Presumably the client has already been looking inward for answers and has not discovered enough to be satisfied. And we are all vulnerable to the egoistic drift toward self-serving conclusions that have little
to do with truth or rationality. The human capacity to justify false beliefs
is humbling and stunning.

Possibility 2 involves the counselor and client working together to determine what is true, rational and moral. This is usually better than the client
being the sole arbiter of truth; two heads are better than one. Using a
method of collaborative empiricism (Beck, 1995), client and counselor can
set up "experiments" to test out the client's beliefs in order to see if they are
valid. But two heads are not always that good either. In cognitive therapy,
most therapists and clients experience a subtle tug toward *functional relativism* (McMinn & Campbell, 2007) where truth is determined based on what
helps reduce the client's symptoms. Truth becomes less important than telling a story that helps bring comfort and hope to the client. This is enough
for some constructivist counselors, but most Christian counselors find this
approach to truth anemic and unsatisfying.

Possibility 3 is that a community of faith helps both the counselor and
Christian client think and choose more clearly than they would on their
own. Though they may or may not attend the same church, if both the
counselor and client are part of a Christian community, it can help them
find consensus on particular ways of thinking and standards of truth.
Christian community functions in two dimensions—historically and contemporaneously. Historically, many faithful saints have walked before us
and dedicated enormous moral and intellectual capacities to understanding and articulating God's truth. The Nicene Creed, for example, is not
merely a citation for Sunday morning worship; it is a succinct articulation
of the Christian faith that was assembled by many brilliant minds in A.D.
325 and revised in the intervening centuries. Enormous wisdom for Christian living can be found in the historical community of faith that precedes
us (Roberts, 2000). Imagine how much richer our Christian experience is
because of biblical authors and those who followed them—Augustine,
Athanasius, John Cassian, Gregory the Great, Thomas Aquinas, John of the
Cross, Teresa of Ávila, Pascal, Jonathan Edwards, Evelyn Underhill, Simone
Weil, Mother Teresa, Henri Nouwen and so many more. The historical

community of faith helps us persevere in the midst of life's trials, fixing our eyes on Christ who is the perfect image of God.

> Therefore, since we are surrounded by such a huge crowd of witnesses to the life of faith, let us strip off every weight that slows us down, especially the sin that so easily trips us up. And let us run with endurance the race God has set before us. We do this by keeping our eyes on Jesus, the champion who initiates and perfects our faith. Because of the joy awaiting him, he endured the cross, disregarding its shame. Now he is seated in the place of honor beside God's throne. Think of all the hostility he endured from sinful people; then you won't become weary and give up. (Heb 12:1-3)

Contemporaneously, being in a Christian community means that we are connected in relationships and accountability with others who walk alongside us in the journey of faith. This helps keep us on track in the midst of the postmodern swirl in which we live. When we remove soul care from the church and place it in the hands of practitioners accountable only to state and federal regulatory bodies, we risk losing an important connection with a community of grace.

Along with biblical counselors, I believe that a Christian community of grace is an important part of Christian soul care—both for the sake of the client and the sake of the counselor. With Christian clients, I find value in each of the three possibilities described above—looking for truth inwardly; client and counselor working together to sharpen the client's reasoning; and looking to a historical and contemporaneous community of faith.

Three Dimensions of Grace

God has given us a great gift. A part of God's very nature has been granted us in the gift of thought. With thought we can understand God's majesty by studying the world around us. We can huddle together in human community and share the language of ideas. We can understand God's revealed Word. As amazing as human structural capacities are, both theology and psychology demonstrate that our thinking is tainted with egoism and often wrong.

We easily turn the gift of human ontology into a curse with our short-sighted pride. We wander away from God and community, using the reasoning skills God gave us to construct arguments denying his relevance. We squander the gift of thought on selfish ambition, trying to convince others that we are right rather than growing in wisdom by hearing what they have to say. We ignore important peripheral information while clinging to that in the center of our vision. We hold fiercely to untenable beliefs even when they are clearly wrong, and we are more confident in our opinions than we ought to be. Instead of using our reasoning for good, we sometimes use it to distance ourselves from God's embrace and to seek false significance by asserting dominance over others.

This is not a call to retreat from thinking. We can celebrate our capacity to think by studying, reading, reasoning, and engaging in rich and lively dialogue with others. But we need to remember that our reasoning is part of our sinful state and thus vulnerable to error. We need each other to help us think better than we might alone, and we need enough humility to admit our need for others.

So how can a Christian counselor respond when a troubled soul is looking for a more reasonable way to understand life? Grace. Grace is experienced in three dimensions when working with clients in the structural domain. First, there is a quiet, accepting grace where the counselor sits in an open, nonjudgmental way, encouraging the client to look inward to explore thought processes, moral commitments and so on. Christian counselors have been touched and transformed by the grace of Christ, so one proper response is to be remarkably gracious to those seeking their help. "Therefore, accept each other just as Christ has accepted you so that God will be given glory" (Rom 15:7). Second, there is an interpersonal grace where counselor and client work together to understand the client's life story and the schemas emerging from the story. Over time, clients learn to distance themselves from old schemas and form new schemas that provide future hope and meaning. This process, described in detail in *Integrative Psychotherapy* (McMinn & Campbell, 2007), shares similarity to the old-self/new-self language found in the apostle Paul's epistles. Third, Christian clients and counselors best function as part of a community of grace. Ideally, the church—both historical and contemporary—helps us sort truth from falsehood and provides spiritual and emotional support as we work to conform our lives to the standards of truth that God has revealed.

> I pray that from his glorious, unlimited resources he will empower you with inner strength through his Spirit. Then Christ will make his home in your hearts as you trust in him. Your roots will grow down into God's love and keep you strong. And may you have the power to understand, as all God's people should, how wide, how long, how high, and how deep his love is. May you experience the love of Christ, though it is too great to understand fully. Then

you will be made complete with all the fullness of life and power that comes from God.

Now all glory to God, who is able, through his mighty power at work within us, to accomplish infinitely more than we might ask or think. Glory to him in the church and in Christ Jesus through all generations forever and ever! Amen. (Eph 3:16-21)

8

Sin and Grace
in the Relational Domain

LISA AND I WERE SITTING AT THE MUSTY, over-the-hill community movie the-ater on a January evening when we noticed flashlight rays bouncing down the middle aisle. They stopped right next to us as I felt a tap on my right shoulder. Two of our three daughters were looking for us: "Dad, Mom, you guys need to leave. Megan is at the police station." That got our attention. It seemed unimaginable that some terrible thing had taken Megan, our de-lightful eighth-grade daughter, to the police station. The unimaginable be-came palpable in the minutes that followed. Megan had privately ventured, or perhaps stumbled, into the world of shoplifting. Thankfully, she wasn't very good and was caught early in her aspiring career. The police arrived, cuffed her, took her to the police station and called our home—where her older sisters took the call and began the quest of finding their parents at the discount movie theater.

We found Megan's repentant and shamed ruins huddled on a wooden bench inside the police station. Her first words, spoken in a voice shaking with sadness and fear, were heartrending and good: "I am so sorry. I am so sorry." We talked to the police officer—a good-hearted man who knew ex-actly how to handle such things—and then left for our silent drive home. Megan walked in the house and went straight to her room to contemplate her shame and her plight. Lisa and I talked for a bit, trying to make sense out of one of the biggest surprises of our lives, and then I went upstairs to say a few words to Megan before bed.

When I got there, words just didn't seem right. So I sat. Megan sat. No words—just silence that seemed too poignant to interrupt with sound. We sat a long time. When I finally got up to leave, I said, "Megan, we will need to talk about consequences tomorrow, after Mom and I have discussed this some more, but for now I was wondering if we could hug." I thought she might resist with the angry defiance that comes in the aftermath of shame, but there was no resistance at all. She stood and clung to me tightly—perhaps as tightly as I grasped her—and we held each other up in one of the most confusing moments of life. It transformed into one of the most cherished moments of my life as she sensed the safety of my embrace and let her tears loose. The tears erupted in heaving sobs of contrition, sorrow and repentance. And then mine came too—tears of lament for my periods of absence in her life, of regret for the darts of criticism I had aimed at Megan over the years, of empathic sorrow for the bitter grief now engulfing her, of uncertainty about what the future would hold and of profound love for this child of mine. There we stood for a long time, two confused sinners, holding on for Megan's life.

That event changed Megan, as defining moments do. Two years after the shoplifting episode Megan told the story to our church congregation before she was baptized. Megan is a seminary student now—the kind of young adult that every parent wishes for—and we recognize that awful January evening to be one of the milestones in her development. She has since given both Lisa and me permission to use the story in our speaking and our writing, reflecting the sort of courage that has always been part of Megan's character.

Megan's story could be told through a functional lens: we are created to be responsible stewards of creation, and when we lapse into episodes of poor self-control, bad things are likely to occur. This is true enough, but it lacks explanatory power. It could be told as a story of structural deficit: Megan's choice to shoplift reflected some deficit in her rational and moral capacities as an eighth-grader. Again, true enough, but her first words at the police station, "I'm so sorry," were not an apology for her lapse in logic but for a breach of relationship. She was saying, "I am so sorry that I offended you and others who love me by doing this unlawful and selfish thing." And when we embraced later that evening, it was no effort to restore functional or structural abilities; it was a relational healing, an affirmation that love triumphs over sin.

Functional and structural problems are consequences of sin, but the essence of sin is relational. When we read of Adam and Eve eating the forbidden fruit (Gen 3:1-7), it is certainly a functional breakdown of their mandate to be stewards over creation, but that is not our greatest concern. Their choice also reflected the tragic assertiveness of an autonomous and arbitrary exercise of volition; structurally, it was disastrous. But again, that is not our greatest concern, nor was it theirs. Most of all, their sin was a relational offense, and so is ours. Adam and Eve chose to defy God, and their immediate response was to experience shame and hide themselves from one another and from God. We are still hiding.

SURVEY SAYS 8.1: The Relational Nature of Sin

Christians sometimes think of sin as violating a list of bad behaviors that ought to be avoided or failing to live up to a list of good behaviors that should be pursued. This is not altogether wrong, of course, because holy living involves both aspirations to pursue and abominations to eschew. But sin is fundamentally a separation from God, refusing to submit to the proper Creator-creature relationship, and its consequences also separate us from one another. When asked what they wished Christian psychologists knew about sin, several of the Christian leaders we surveyed noted the profound relational consequences of sin.

> The devastating emotional and physical effects on persons and on all their relationships.

> That, fundamentally, humans are fallen persons with impaired capacities to love and serve God and other persons.

> Specifically how it militates against humility in intimate or conflicted relationships and how it blocks the ability to take ownership of specific contributions to the problems.

Just as sin is relational, so is grace. The power of the gospel is seen in restored relationship, with Creator and creature restored through the work of Jesus Christ.

> When we were utterly helpless, Christ came at just the right time and died for us sinners. Now, most people would not be willing to die for an upright person, though someone might perhaps be willing to die for a person who is especially good. But God showed his great love for us by sending Christ to die for us while we were still sinners. And since we have been made right in God's sight by the blood of Christ, he will certainly save us from God's condemnation. For since our friendship with God was restored by the death of his Son while we were still his enemies, we will certainly be saved through the life of his Son. So now we can rejoice in our wonderful new relationship with God because our Lord Jesus Christ has made us friends of God. (Rom 5:6-11)

We misunderstand sin when we think of it only as violating a principle of moral goodness. Sin is stronger, much stronger, than any list of behavioral or attitudinal violations. Sin involves rebellion, breaking away from God, insisting that our desires and will are more important than God's. And if sin is fundamentally a relational issue, so is grace. Grace involves an amazing amount of forgiveness, but it is even bigger than forgiveness. Grace justifies us before a holy God and sanctifies us too, as we grow to become more like the fully functioning humans we were created to be. That is, grace allows us to become more like Christ.

Jesus told a story about a prodigal son (Lk 15:11-32) where a young man squanders his inheritance on loose living; when faced with starvation or repentance, he chooses to turn back toward home. The power of the story is in restored relationship. We don't read the story and say, "Oh good, at least he will have something to eat now." No, we are choked up by the beauty of love. That which was shattered by selfish ambition and relational sin is now redeemed by the repentance of the son and the gracious response of a loving father. As the father and son embrace, so our personal disappointments with strained relationships embrace the possibility of forgiveness and healing. We cling to the hope that the end of the Christian journey is found in the embrace of an all-knowing Creator who loves beyond what any word can express. It is a perfect love, the kind the New Testament writer John knew "expels all fear" (1 Jn 4:18).

Relationality in Integrative Psychotherapy

A Christian psychologist fresh out of graduate school once told me that if people suddenly stopped having relational crises, he would no longer have a practice. Sadly, he is in no danger of losing his practice because relational challenge and failure is part of the human journey. We may envision a day when relationships are completely pure and good, but that is another day. Today we live in a broken place where we disappoint and misunderstand one another. Relationships have problems, hearts are broken, marriages are splintered and children are devastated. We long for the sort of grace that restores and heals us, or at least brings hope and comfort when full healing seems beyond reach.

The third domain of Integrative Psychotherapy (McMinn & Campbell, 2007) focuses on the relational nature of wounds and healing (figure 8.1). Clients who persist long enough and probe deep enough in counseling are likely to discover relational roots to their ongoing struggles and longings. Maladaptive schemas (discussed in chapter seven) do not merely emerge from faulty reasoning; they result from formative relationships in a person's life. Past relationships are then reenacted in the present, producing patterns that lead some people to counseling:

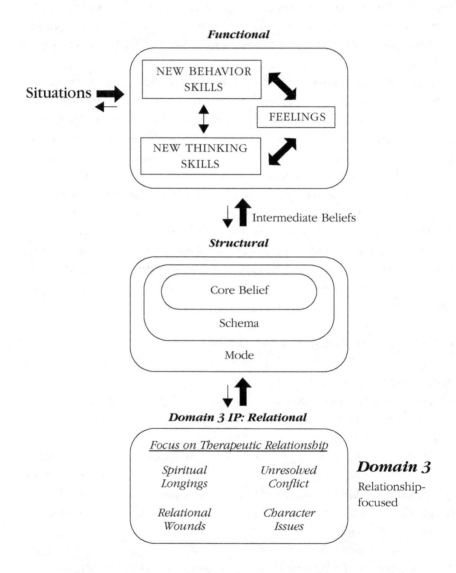

Figure 8.1. Relational domain interventions involve healing relational wounds (adapted from McMinn & Campbell, 2007).

1. A middle-aged executive who struggles with anger and stress discovers how she is reenacting an obsession with competence that was initially fostered in relation to her father who told her she would never amount to anything.

2. A depressed, helpless man recognizes how his dependency relationship with his doting mother affects his current expectations in marriage and friendship.

3. The woman feeling aloof and distant from God recognizes a similar feeling from childhood, with parents who were so busy with careers that they had little time for their children.

4. The man struggling with sexual compulsions recognizes the depth of his longing for intimacy and connection and how poorly these longings were met in his abusive home.

It would be easy to look at these examples and conclude that all psychological problems should be attributed to parents. But this is far too simplistic. Every parent recognizes how difficult parenting can be, and every Christian

---

COUNSELING TIP 8.1: *Avoiding the Victim Role*

There is an implicit challenge in relational counseling: we want our clients to explore the painful experiences that occurred earlier in life, yet we don't want those explorations to calcify into bitterness and resentment. In other words, we want our clients to be honest about the past without seeing themselves as victims who are destined to be miserable as a result of past offenses. Most often these offenses involve parents or other caregivers.

One helpful strategy is to offer passing comments or subtle words of understanding or affirmation regarding the caregiver even as the client is making connections with events of the past. For example:

"I'm sure your father was trying to be helpful to you with some of his comments, but it ended up feeling far more critical than helpful."

"We talked about your relationship with your parents last week. We don't want to vilify them in any way—being a parent is a tough job—but what we were discussing last week also seems related to what you are saying today, about how hard it is for you to feel important and valued by others."

These examples give the client permission to probe the past while attempting to keep the client out of an embittered victim role.

recognizes—or ought to—how pervasively sin affects us all. Psychological wounds emerge from a complex web of biological, social, familial and spiritual factors. And if wounds are complex, so is healing. Effective Christian counseling is more complex than simply prescribing medication, changing a person's thinking processes, promoting behavioral change, enhancing spiritual disciplines or engaging in some cathartic exploration of repressed childhood emotions. Counseling is a nuanced relationship where healing is promoted in multiple dimensions—behavioral, cognitive, social, spiritual, biological and so on. The relational domain of Integrative Psychotherapy explores how to craft an optimal relationship between counselor and client so that healing can occur, considering the grace and truth revealed in Jesus (Jn 1:14) as well as psychological dynamics such as interpersonal processes, cyclical maladaptive patterns and reciprocal role procedures.

Sin and Grace in Three Dimensions

In chapter two, we considered three dimensions of sin—sinfulness, sins and consequences of sin—each of which has profound implications for our relationships with one another and with God, and for counseling. In this chapter we will consider how a posture of grace can be expressed in Christian counseling for each dimension of human sin.

Grace and sinfulness. Sinfulness has to do with our general state of brokenness—it is part of our original condition as fallen human beings. In our sinful state, we naturally twist perceptions to our own advantage, elevate ourselves above God and others, and misperceive things to support our self-serving inclinations. We are bent, stooped under the weight of sin, and in our crookedness we struggle with relationships. Two people look at the same situation and experience conflict. Sometimes this conflict simply reflects two different personalities, but other times the conflict comes because each is viewing it from a self-serving vantage point. In our sinfulness, we also struggle to relate to God properly. Instead of finding our greatest significance in God's choice to love us, we form unhealthy attachments and obsessions with people and things that ultimately leave us grasping and lusting for more. From a monastery in New York on Ash Wednesday of 1979, Henri J. M. Nouwen—a priest and well-known author on Christian spirituality—cried out to God: "There is so much in me that needs to die: false attachments, greed and anger, impatience and stinginess. O Lord, I am self-centered, concerned about myself, my career, my future, my name and fame" (Nouwen, 1981, p. 24). Nouwen's words strike with poignancy and relevance as he interweaves his desire for God with a description of his ongoing struggle with pride, and it's not difficult to recognize his struggle in ourselves. We so easily build idols of the heart, clinging to the wrong relationships—or to the right relationships for the wrong motives—or using our attachments to people to avoid our deeper yearning for God. Or perhaps we give up on people and God altogether and slip into the world of attachments to things: investment accounts, cars, cocaine, reputations, gambling, houses, careers, sex or alcohol. Saint John of the Cross, a sixteenth-century Carmelite monk, noted that false attachments "weary, torment, darken, defile and weaken [the soul]" (John of the Cross, 1584/1991, p. 132).

Our common state of sinfulness calls for empathy in Christian counseling. We do not sit above our clients; we sit with them, familiar with the pain of broken relationships, the struggle of disordered passions and the hope of redemption. This is an existential sort of empathy, not merely a technique-oriented empathy. In other words, it is good to lean forward when a client is conveying a difficult and painful story, but it is not enough. Empathy rooted in grace also calls us to an inner identification with every struggle and pain of living. We are aboard the same misguided ship—misdirected and confused and trying to find our bearings. This is a humble posture, recognizing that no counselor, save the Wonderful Counselor (Is 9:6), has been fully rescued from the distortions of sinfulness.

Cara is a twenty-one-year-old university student who comes for counseling after an unsuccessful suicide attempt. She is depressed, disoriented and confused about the direction of her life. When asked about family history of psychiatric disorder, she mentions that her mother and maternal grandfather both had "breakdowns" that involved hospitalizations and electroconvulsive therapy. Her mother—from whom Cara is estranged—is still on a low dosage of antidepressant medication. Cara had a Christian conversion experience in high school and became quite involved in her church youth group and summer missions trips. She describes her faith as important to her, though she has wandered from her moral commitments since beginning at the university three years ago. She is sexually promiscuous, drinking alcohol regularly and excessively, and using illegal drugs occasionally.

The competent Christian counselor's first impulse in working with Cara will be one of empathy and compassion (see table 8.1). Though her counselor may have never veered as far off track as Cara has, the counselor can at least recognize the propensity to wander away from God's will. "All of us, like sheep, have strayed away. / We have left God's paths to follow our own" (Is 53:6). Without the grace of God, revealed in our Lord Jesus Christ, none of us would have a chance of favor with God.

Further, the counselor will suspect the possibility of biological predisposition to depression—another manifestation of human brokenness. With two close relatives having experienced severe depression, Cara may be prone to it also. And the relational fabric of Cara's life will also be a concern to the counselor. She is estranged from her mother, and her promiscuity suggests an unfulfilled yearning for intimacy. With an attitude of compassion and empathy, a Christian counselor can be a voice of stability, grace and gentle care in Cara's life.

Grace and sins. A gracious, empathic presence with Cara will be essential, but virtually any counselor can provide this. Why did Cara choose a Christian counselor? Perhaps in the aftermath of a suicide attempt she is looking for someone who will help her reclaim her faith values and set her in a better direction with her life. Maybe she is looking for a repentance-friendly relationship where grace and truth are both evident.

It is not only our general state of brokenness that hinders our Christian walk and impedes relationships; it is also our sinful misdirection. This is a simple truth that we have sometimes neglected in Christian psychology. Perhaps it sounds too much like fundamentalism to connect sin with the damage it causes, or too much like prosperity gospel to associate obedience with spiritual intimacy. I agree that great damage has been caused by those who make simplistic connections between personal behavior and well-being, but to deny the connection altogether seems inane. When I behave in a selfish and sinful way toward someone I love, the relationship suffers as a result. This also holds true in my relationship with God. God has lovingly provided us with instruction for living well, so that we may experience life-giving, enriching relationships with God and neighbor. When I put self-interest ahead of loving God, I behave as Adam and Eve did in the creation account. Adam and Eve covered themselves and hid in their shame, so also my sin separates me from close fellowship with God and others. Throughout Scripture we see God making clear connections between choices and relationship, and we encounter the call to repent of our sinful choices and to turn back to our relational covenants. We see this throughout the Old Testament as God related to the chosen people of Israel. For example, God appeared to Solomon after he completed the Temple, reminding him:

> Then if my people who are called by my name will humble themselves and
> pray and seek my face and turn from their wicked ways, I will hear from
> heaven and will forgive their sins and restore their land. My eyes will be open
> and my ears attentive to every prayer made in this place. (2 Chron 7:14-15)

In the New Testament we continue to see calls to repentance *(metanoia)*
and renewed relationship with God. The classic parable of the prodigal son
in Luke 15 is about God pursuing those who are lost, but God's pursuit of
lost people is always intertwined with human agency. The prodigal, faced
with starvation, eventually "came to his senses" (Lk 15:17) and headed back
toward home. His repentance made possible a renewed relationship with
his gracious father.

Throughout each of our lives we have opportunity to repent, turn back
from our sin and head down the dusty path toward home (McMinn, 2005).
And when we do, it has emotional and psychological implications as well
as spiritual. I have witnessed the cleansing power of confession and the
beauty of healed relationship many times in my years as a psychologist.
Each time I am deeply moved by the splendor of grace; it resonates with
some unnamed primordial cadence in the human soul. Those who are able
to confess and forgive are often transported beyond the limits of what they
thought possible, and the healing that ensues takes my breath away: express-
sions of remorse, tears of loss and joy, and the beautiful gift of humility. If
it were not for repentance and forgiveness, every person and every relationship would eventually accumulate into a mountain of bitterness and resentment. Living in grace-filled relationships means recognizing and repenting
of our sins and forgiving others for theirs: "Make allowance for each other's
faults, and forgive anyone who offends you. Remember, the Lord forgave
you, so you must forgive others" (Col 3:13).

The essence of grace in Christian counseling involves a compassionate
acceptance—recognizing that we all make sinful choices—coupled with a
vision for right living. A repentance-friendly environment (see figure 8.1) is
one in which the client feels safe and accepted, yet remains open to being
challenged and convicted by the Holy Spirit. Just as God's grace toward us
is both justifying and sanctifying, so we ought to treat one another with both
tender acceptance and encouragement toward righteousness. Both are central to Christian counseling. I look to the biblical counselors with admiration
in this regard. Though they are often caricatured as intolerant fanatics who

make simplistic connections between sanctified living and psychopathology, this has not been my experience with most biblical counselors. Most attempt to balance interpersonal kindness with their love for holiness. David Powlison, who has been a key figure at the Christian Counseling and Educational Foundation, is one of the kindest and most gracious individuals I have ever known. Yet he also stands for the importance of holy living. David

---

COUNSELING TIP 8.2: *Repentance in Twelve-Step Programs*

Christian counselors have a variety of reactions to the twelve-step recovery model. Many of these programs speak of a higher power without acknowledging God's personal and loving nature, for example. But Christians can celebrate many aspects of twelve-step programs, including the emphasis on repentance. Notice the centrality of repentance in steps four through ten:

1. We admitted we were powerless over our addiction—that our lives had become unmanageable

2. Came to believe that a Power greater than ourselves could restore us to sanity

3. Made a decision to turn our will and our lives over to the care of God as we understood God

4. Made a searching and fearless moral inventory of ourselves

5. Admitted to God, to ourselves and to another human being the exact nature of our wrongs

6. Were entirely ready to have God remove all these defects of character

7. Humbly asked God to remove our shortcomings

8. Made a list of all persons we had harmed, and became willing to make amends to them all

9. Made direct amends to such people wherever possible, except when to do so would injure them or others

10. Continued to take personal inventory and when we were wrong promptly admitted it

11. Sought through prayer and meditation to improve our conscious contact with God as we understood God, praying only for knowledge of God's will for us and the power to carry that out

12. Having had a spiritual awakening as the result of these steps, we tried to carry this message to other addicts, and to practice these principles in all our affairs. (12step.org, 2006)

is a wonderful picture of grace and truth; I know he has blessed many counselors and counseling clients over his career.

As much as I admire how most biblical counselors handle issues of personal sin in counseling, some biblical counselors focus on personal sin without paying adequate attention to the other two dimensions of sin: our general state of brokenness (sinfulness) and the consequences of sin that stem from early life relationships. Perhaps they make this error to compensate for the integrationist movement, which has paid too little attention to personal sin (Monroe, 2001). A relational view of sin and grace calls us to look at all three dimensions of sin and to consider the gift of grace in relation to the larger social milieu in which every human functions.

Grace and the consequences of sin. Cara is weighed down by a general state of brokenness, by her personal choices that have taken her astray from an abundant life of obedience and also by the consequences of others' sin. She recalls being teased and ridiculed in school because of a minor speech impediment. Her mother—single at the time—could not afford speech therapy. Cara's impediment—and the teasing—continued through her elementary school years. Between the ages of thirteen and sixteen she was sexually abused by her stepfather. When her mother and stepfather later divorced, Cara disclosed the abuse to her mother. Cara was shocked to learn that her mother had suspected abuse all along yet had not intervened. At times it seemed that her mother blamed Cara for the divorce. Cara and her mother have had virtually no contact over the past three years.

Sin has weighty consequences that extend into future generations. Cara lives in a lonely world as a result of how others have treated her. She is bound by a maladaptive schema: "I am unacceptable, different and alone, and my only hope of connection is to be who others want me to be." This schema emerged from the relational texture of Cara's life, and it continues to have a profound effect on her relationships today. Her promiscuity, for example, is not only a sinful choice that she makes; it is also a consequence of others' sins against her.

Effective Christian counselors customize therapeutic relationships to address the particular schemas that shape their clients' outlook on life (see figure 8.1). In Cara's case, she feels that she can only be acceptable if she does what others want her to do. She will naturally slip into the same role in relation to her counselor, so it will be important for the counselor to avoid too many direct suggestions. Though Cara may be compliant if her counselor gives specific prescriptions—stop drinking so much, spend more time doing school work, don't sleep around and so on—the greater healing will only occur if Cara can discover an internalized moral voice rather than simply trying to please her counselor. Early on, her counselor

---

IN THE OFFICE 8.1: Repentance-Friendly Counseling

Counselors do not need to be forceful in order to create an environment for clients to evaluate their lives and acknowledge misconduct. In fact, an overly direct approach may make the client defensive and less likely to admit fault. It is generally more useful to probe with reflections and queries that may foster conviction. For example:

Ralph: It's none of her business. I'm just tired of her whining.

Mark: Ralph, when you say it's none of Melissa's business where you go after work, I hear you saying that you would like her to stop questioning you as soon as you get home.

Ralph: Yeah, it's like getting interrogated every time I walk in the door.

Mark: I can see how that would be difficult.

Ralph: It's terrible.

Mark: I'm wondering, though, how literally to take you when you say it is none of her business what you do with your time.

Ralph: Well, if I want to stop off for a drink or stay and talk with a colleague over the water cooler, I'm a grown man and I should be able to do it.

Mark: Yes, I see your perspective on that. How do you suppose Melissa hears it when you say it's none of her business?

Ralph: She doesn't like it.

Mark: That makes sense. How do you suppose it feels to her?

Ralph: Maybe like I'm putting a wall between us or something.

Mark: So your intent is to keep from feeling interrogated, but the way you do it ends up building a wall between you and Melissa.

Ralph: Yeah, I guess it does. There must be a better way for us to talk about this.

Mark: Yes, I agree. We can work on that.

will need to function as a coach, encouraging and nudging Cara in healthy directions while avoiding any sort of verbal or nonverbal expressions that communicate, "Do this or I won't be pleased." Later, after enough rapport and trust have been built, Cara's counselor may deliberately express some disappointment while still accepting and acting kindly toward Cara. This will disturb Cara at first, because she will want to please her counselor, but it will ultimately help her gain greater distance from her schema as she begins to realize that her acceptability is not contingent on the counselor's approval.

Healing relationships look different with different clients. Sometimes counselors need to be quite unimpressed with a client's achievements because the client has built a personal identity around accomplishment. Other times a counselor needs to be firm and direct as the client learns to release an unhealthy need for control. Each counseling relationship is different, and each can be an expression of grace to a person who is trying to gain insight and distance from the painful consequences of another's sin.

Dimension of Sin	Grace in Christian Counseling
Sinfulness	Empathic Relationship
Sins	Repentence-Friendly Relationship
Consequences of Sin	Healing Relationship

Figure 8.1. Dimensions of sin and grace in Christian counseling

An Integrated View of Christian Counseling

I began this book by pointing out the false distinction between "sin-focused biblical counselors" and "grace-focused Christian psychologists." Such a distinction does injustice to biblical counselors and overstates the extent of grace evident in Christian psychology. Sin and grace are part of the same story, and if either is split off from the other the result is something far less than the good news of Christianity. I have attempted to write an integrative book even as I have been critical of some of the integrationists' perspectives. Sin and grace should be held together. So should psychology and theology. So should grace and truth.

When counselors get together, they tend to divide themselves according to theoretical perspectives. Theologians do the same. And when theologians get together with counselors, feathers fly. My hope is that this small book will help Christians move together under the banner of God's grace.

Most counseling models fit into one of three categories. Acceptance-focused counseling is based on the assumption that people have been wounded through past relationships and that a corrective relational experience will help them heal. Contemporary humanistic and object-relations counselors operate with this understanding. Skills-focused counseling assumes that people struggle because they lack particular cognitive or behavioral skills to manage the complexity of their lives. Behavioral and cognitive-behavioral counselors work on this premise. Moral counseling assumes that people are troubled because they have drifted or darted away from proper living and are suffering as a result. They need to be redirected to get back on the right path. Some pastoral, biblical and nouthetic counselors have emphasized moral counseling. All three of these strategies are good if woven together, but they are potentially damaging and misleading if viewed apart from the other two.

Acceptance is a virtuous way to treat people and one that is consistent with how Christ taught us to be with one another. But acceptance without direction contributes to a therapeutic culture that seems content to discard truth—or at least to leave it vague and undefined. Skills are important; they help people cope and find peace in the midst of life's turmoil. But teaching skills without compassion overlooks the relational nature of our wounds and of healing, and skills without moral substance easily devolve into functional relativism—truth is defined by whatever makes someone feel better. Moral guidance is essential (and counselors always offer it whether or not they know or admit it), but if moral guidance is offered without relational sensitivity the result can be more *de*moralizing than moralizing. And giving moral guidance without teaching skills is suggesting people change without helping them know *how* to change. Acceptance and skills and moral guidance are all essential facets of Christian counseling. They come together at the intersection of grace and truth.

The Christian story is a story of relationship: a relational God—Father, Son and Holy Spirit—created relational humans to thrive in the context of intimacy. Sin is our great obstacle, keeping us far from God and distancing us from one another. Sin and the damage it causes reverberate in each human soul, every human community and all cultures. We are a people in need of grace. Praise be to God who is utterly consistent and faithful, who so desires relationship with humanity that Christ entered our mire to live among us, to bear our sin and to restore that which is broken by sin. Herein is our great hope as Christians: Christ in us, the hope of glory (see Col 1:27). We Christian counselors have the tremendous privilege of being ambassadors of hope, believing that God's reconciling and transforming grace is always at work.

References

12Step.org. (2006). *The 12 Steps* [On-line]. Retrieved August 11, 2006. Available: www.12step.org/steps/index.php

Adams, J. E. (1970). *Competent to counsel*. Grand Rapids, MI: Baker Books.

Augustine of Hippo. (1986). *The confessions of St. Augustine* (H. M. Helms, Trans.). Brewster, MA: Paraclete. (Original work published 398)

Beck, J. S. (1995). *Cognitive therapy: Basics and beyond*. New York: Guilford.

Benner, D. G. (2005). *The gift of being yourself: The sacred call to self-discovery*. Downers Grove, IL: InterVarsity Press.

Bennett, A. (Ed.). (1975). *The valley of vision: A collection of Puritan prayers & devotions*. Carlisle, PA: Banner of Truth Trust.

Berkouwer, G. C. (1971). *Studies in dogmatics: Sin*. Grand Rapids, MI: Eerdmans.

Blamires, H. (1963). *The Christian mind: How should a Christian think?* Ann Arbor, MI: Servant.

Bloesch, D. G. (1978). *Essentials of evangelical theology: God, authority, and salvation* (Vol. 1). Peabody, MA: Prince.

Bonhoeffer, D. (1959). *The cost of discipleship* (Rev. ed.). New York: Macmillan.

Bowlby, J. (1990). *A secure base: Parent-child attachment and healthy human development*. New York: Basic Books.

Butler, A. C., Chapman, J. E., Forman, E. M., & Beck, A. T. (2006). The empirical status of cognitive-behavioral therapy: A review of meta-analyses. *Clinical Psychology Review, 26*, 17-31.

Charry, E. T. (2001). Theology after psychology. In M. R. McMinn & T. R. Phillips (Eds.), *Care for the soul: Exploring the interface of psychology & theology* (pp. 118-33). Downers Grove, IL: InterVarsity Press.

Christian History Institute. (2004). John Newton, servant of slaves, discovers amazing grace! [On-line]. *Glimpses Bulletin Inserts, Issue #28*. Retrieved January 18, 2006. Available: chi.gospelcom.net/GLIMPSEF/Glimpses/glmps028.shtml

Crabb, L. (2002). *The pressure's off: There's a new way to live*. Colorado Springs: Waterbrook.

Edwards, J. (1996). *Religious affections: A Christian's character before God* (J. M. Houston, Ed.). Minneapolis: Bethany House. (Original work published 1746)

Eitzen, D. S., & Zinn, M. B. (2003). *Social problems* (9th ed.). Boston: Allyn and Bacon.

Ellis, A. (1960). There is no place for the concept of sin in psychotherapy. *Journal of Counseling Psychology, 7,* 192.

Ellis, A. (1971). *The case against religion: A psychotherapist's view.* New York: Institute for Rational Living.

Ellis, A. (2000). Can Rational Emotive Behavior Therapy (REBT) be effectively used with people who have devout beliefs in God and religion? *Professional Psychology: Research and Practice, 31,* 29-33.

Epley, N., & Dunning, D. (2000). Feeling "holier than thou": Are self-serving assessments produced by errors in self- or social prediction? *Journal of Personality and Social Psychology, 79,* 861-75.

Epstein, S. (1994). Integration of the cognitive and the psychodynamic unconscious. *American Psychologist, 49,* 709-24.

Erickson, M. J. (1985). *Christian theology.* Grand Rapids, MI: Baker Book House.

Foster, R. J. (1992). *Prayer: Finding the heart's true home.* San Francisco: HarperCollins.

Foster, R. J. (1995). In J. B. Smith, *Embracing the love of God: The path and promise of Christian life.* San Francisco: HarperSanFrancisco.

Foster, R. J. (1998). *Streams of living water: Celebrating the great traditions of Christian faith.* San Francisco: HarperSanFrancisco.

Grenz, S. J. (2000). *Renewing the center: Evangelical theology in a post-theological era.* Grand Rapids, MI: Baker Academic.

Hoekema, A. A. (1986). *Created in God's image.* Grand Rapids, MI: Eerdmans.

Hugo, V. (1997). *Les Misérables* (C. E. Wilbour, Trans.). New York: Knopf.

John of the Cross. (1991). *The collected works of St. John of the Cross* (K. Kavanaugh & O. Rodriguez, Trans.). Washington, DC: Institute of Carmelite Studies, 1991. (Original work published approximately 1584)

Jones, E. E., & Pulos, S. M. (1993). Comparing the process in psychodynamic and cognitive-behavioral therapies. *Journal of Consulting and Clinical Psychology, 61,* 306-16.

Jones, L. G. (1995). *Embodying forgiveness: A theological analysis.* Grand Rapids, MI: Eerdmans.

Jones, S. L. (1994). A constructive relationship for religion within the science and profession of psychology: Perhaps the boldest model yet. *American Psychologist, 49,* 184-99.

Jones, S. L., & Butman, R. E. (1991). *Modern psychotherapies: A comprehensive Christian appraisal.* Downers Grove, IL: InterVarsity Press.

Kimnach, W. H., Minkema, K. P., & Sweeney, D. A. (Eds.). (1999). *The sermons of Jonathan Edwards: A reader.* New Haven, CT: Yale University Press.

Koocher, G. P. (2006, April). On being there. *Monitor on Psychology,* 5-6.

Lambert, M. J. (1992). Implications of outcome research for psychotherapy integration. In J. C. Norcross & M. R. Goldfried (Eds.), *Handbook of psychotherapy integration* (pp. 94-129). New York: Basic Books.

Lambert, M. J. (Ed). (2004). *Bergin & Garfield's handbook of psychotherapy and behavior change* (5th ed.). New York: Wiley.

Lambert, M. J., & Barley, D. E. (2002). Research summary on the therapeutic relationship and psychotherapy outcome. In John C. Norcross (Ed.), *Psychotherapy relationships that work* (pp. 17-32). New York: Oxford.

Lewis, C. S. (1952). *Mere Christianity* (Rev. ed.). New York: Macmillan.

Martin, B. (1950). *John Newton: A biography.* London: Heinemann.

May, G. G. (1988). *Addiction & grace: Love and spirituality in the healing of addictions.* New York: HarperCollins.

McMinn, M. R. (1996). *Psychology, theology, and spirituality in Christian counseling.* Wheaton, IL: Tyndale.

McMinn, M. R. (2005). *Finding our way home: Turning back to what matters most.* San Francisco: Jossey-Bass.

McMinn, M. R. (2006). *Christian Counseling* [DVD in APA Psychotherapy Video Series]. Washington, DC: American Psychological Association.

McMinn, M. R., & Campbell, C. D. (2007). *Integrative psychotherapy: Toward a comprehensive Christian approach.* Downers Grove, IL: IVP Academic.

McMinn, M. R., & Dominguez, A. D. (Eds.). (2005). *Psychology and the church.* Hauppauge, NY: Nova Science Publishers.

McMinn, M. R., Meek, K. R., Canning, S. S., & Pozzi, C. F. (2001). Training psychologists to work with religious organizations: The Center for Church-Psychology Collaboration. *Professional Psychology: Research and Practice, 32,* 324-28.

McMinn, M. R., Ruiz, J. N., Marx, D., Wright, J. B., & Gilbert, N. B. (2006). Professional psychology and the doctrines of sin and grace: Christian leaders' perspectives. *Professional Psychology: Research and Practice, 37,* 295-302.

McWilliams, N. (1994). *Psychoanalytic diagnosis: Understanding personality structure in the clinical process.* New York: Guilford.

Menninger, K. (1973). *Whatever became of sin?* New York: Hawthorn Books.

Miller, D. (2003). *Blue like jazz: Nonreligious thoughts on Christian spirituality.* Nashville: Thomas Nelson.

Monroe, P. G. (1997). Building bridges with biblical counselors. *Journal of Psychology and Theology, 25,* 28-37.

Monroe, P. G. (2001). Exploring client's personal sin in the therapeutic context: Theological perspectives on a case study of self-deceit. In M. R. McMinn & T. R. Phillips (Eds.), *Care for the soul: Exploring the intersection of psychology & theology* (pp. 202-17). Downers Grove, IL: InterVarsity Press.

Moroney, S. K. (2000). *The noetic effects of sin*. Lanham, MA: Lexington Books.

Nouwen, H. J. M. (1972). *The wounded healer*. New York: Doubleday.

Nouwen, H. J. M. (1981). *A Cry for Mercy: Prayers from the Genesee*. New York: Image.

Nouwen, H. J. M. (1992). *Life of the beloved: Spiritual living in a secular world*. New York: Crossroad.

O'Donahue, W. (1989). The (even) bolder model: The clinical psychologist as meta-physician-scientist-practitioner. *American Psychologist, 44*, 1460-68.

Okholm, D. L. (2001). To vent or not to vent? What contemporary psychology can learn from ascetic theology about anger. In M. R. McMinn & T. R. Phillips (Eds.), *Care for the soul: Exploring the interface of psychology & theology* (pp. 164-86). Downers Grove, IL: InterVarsity Press.

Packer, J. I. (1973). *Knowing God*. Downers Grove, IL: InterVarsity Press.

Packer, J. I. (1993). *Concise theology: A guide to historic Christian beliefs*. Wheaton, IL: Tyndale.

Palmer, P. J. (2000). *Let your life speak: Listening for the voice of vocation*. San Francisco: Jossey-Bass.

Pascal, B. (1966). *Pensees* (A. J. Krailsheimer, Trans.). New York: Penguin. (Original work published 1660)

Peterson, C., & Seligman, M. E. P. (2004). *Character strengths and virtues: A handbook and classification*. New York: Oxford University Press.

Peterson, E. H. (1980). *A long obedience in the same direction: Discipleship in an instant society*. Downers Grove, IL: InterVarsity Press.

Plantinga, A. (2000). *Warranted Christian belief*. New York: Oxford University Press.

Plantinga, C., Jr. (1995). *Not the way it's supposed to be: A breviary of sin*. Grand Rapids, MI: Eerdmans.

Powlison, D. (2000). A biblical counseling view. In E. L. Johnson & S. L. Jones (Eds.), *Psychology & Christianity: Four views* (pp. 196-225). Downers Grove, IL: InterVarsity Press.

Powlison, D. (2001). Questions at the crossroads: The care of souls & modern psychotherapies. In M. R. McMinn & T. R. Phillips (Eds.), *Care for the soul: Exploring the intersection of psychology & theology* (pp. 23-61). Downers Grove, IL: InterVarsity Press.

Roberts, R. C., (2000). A Christian psychology view. In E. L. Johnson & S. L. Jones (Eds.), *Psychology & Christianity: Four views* (pp. 148-95). Downers Grove, IL: InterVarsity Press.

Roberts, R. C. (2001). Outline of Pauline psychotherapy. In M. R. McMinn & T. R. Phillips (Eds.), *Care for the soul: Exploring the interface of psychology & theology* (pp. 134-63). Downers Grove, IL: InterVarsity Press.

Robins, R. W., Gosling, S. D., & Craik, K. H. (1999). An empirical analysis of trends in psychology. *American Psychologist, 54,* 117-28.

Rolheiser, R. (1999). *The holy longing: The search for a Christian spirituality.* New York: Doubleday.

Shults, F. L., & Sandage, S. J. (2003). *The faces of forgiveness: Searching for wholeness and salvation.* Grand Rapids, MI: Baker Academic.

Smith, J. B. (1995). *Embracing the love of God: The path and promise of Christian life.* San Francisco: HarperSanFrancisco.

Solzhenitsyn, A. I. (2002). *The Gulag archipelago: 1918-1956* (Abridged by E. E. Ericson Jr.). New York: HarperCollins. (Original work published 1973)

Tangney, J. P. (1991). Moral affect: The good, the bad, and the ugly. *Journal of Personality and Social Psychology, 61,* 598-607.

Tangney, J. P., & Dearing, R. L. (2002). *Shame and guilt.* New York: Guilford.

Taylor, B. B. (2000). *Speaking of sin: The lost language of salvation.* Boston: Cowley.

Taylor, J. (1988). *Holy living* (Updated by Hal M. Helms). Brewster, MA: Paraclete Press. (Original work published 1650)

World Bank Group. (2006). Key development data and statistics [Online]. Retrieved May 23, 2006. Available: www.worldbank.org.

Worthington, E. L., Jr. (2003). *Forgiving and reconciling: Bridges to wholeness and hope.* Downers Grove, IL: InterVarsity Press.

Worthington, E. L., Jr. (Ed.). (2005). *Handbook of forgiveness.* New York: Routledge.

Young, J. E., Klosko, J. S., & Weishaar, M. E. (2003). *Schema therapy: A practitioner's guide.* New York: Guilford.

Name Index

Adams, Jay, 15, 16, 164

apostle Paul, 24, 57, 59, 65, 109, 118, 121, 123, 130, 146

Athanasius, 144

Augustine, 23, 36, 37, 46, 58, 91, 116, 144, 164

Barth, Karl, 81, 98, 100

Berkouwer, G. C., 63, 121, 136, 164

Blamires, Harry, 116, 164

Bloesch, Donald, 40, 164

Bonhoeffer, Dietrich, 62, 63, 164

Brunner, Emil, 98

Burge, Gary, 92

Campbell, Clark, 12, 23, 97, 101, 108, 130, 131, 144, 146, 151, 152, 166

Carlson, Jon, 73

Cassian, John, 116, 144

Crabb, Larry, 64, 164

David, King, 23, 67

Descartes, René, 135

Edwards, Jonathan, 76, 89, 119, 125, 144, 164, 166

Elwell, Walter, 58, 92

Epstein, Seymour, 76, 165

Erickson, Millard, 22, 39, 165

Foster, Richard, 48, 55, 143, 153, 160, 165

Freud, Anna, 51

Freud, Sigmund, 51

Gregory the Great, 116, 144

Hugo, Victor, 65, 66, 165

Jesus, 12, 23, 24, 30, 52, 55, 57, 62, 71, 81, 82, 84, 85, 86, 93, 99, 100, 109, 111, 115, 121, 145, 147, 150, 151, 154, 156

John of the Cross, 144, 155, 165

Koocher, Gerald, 84, 166

Lewis, C. S., 116, 166

May, Gerald, 70, 166

McFerrin, Bobby, 69

Menninger, Karl, 18, 19, 31, 166

Miller, Donald, 60, 61, 166

Monroe, Philip, 15, 16, 24, 26, 109, 159, 166

Murray, Andrew, 116

Newton, John, 26, 27, 28, 29, 30, 31, 58, 164, 166

Nouwen, Henri J. M., 35, 77, 87, 88, 114, 144, 154, 155, 167

Packer, J. I., 40, 59, 62, 167

Palmer, Parker, 68, 69, 70, 71, 84, 167

Pascal, Blaise, 38, 122, 144, 167

Pelagius, 37, 46, 58

Plantinga, Alvin, 39, 42, 105, 116, 136, 167

Powlison, David, 141, 158, 167

Rolheiser, Ronald, 88, 168

Smith, Adam, 44

Smith, James Bryan, 90, 165, 168

Solzhenitsyn, Aleksandr, 38, 168

Taylor, Barbara Brown, 32, 112, 168

Taylor, Jeremy, 42, 168

Teresa, Mother, 84, 144

Teresa of Ávila, 144

Thomas Aquinas, 53, 116, 144

Underhill, Evelyn, 144

Weil, Simone, 144

Whitefield, George, 28, 29

Worthington, Everett, 45, 46, 168

Subject Index

12-steps, 158
ABAB research design, 127
abuse, 18, 42, 44, 50, 59, 105, 113, 115, 122, 159
acceptance, 16, 18, 52, 54, 62, 65, 82, 90, 111, 114, 122, 128, 140, 146, 157, 161, 162
acceptance-focused counseling, 162
accusation, 30, 36, 58, 65, 78, 114, 124, 141
addiction, 23, 50, 70, 84, 86, 105, 158
adversarial approach, 36, 118, 135
affections, 39, 115
ageism, 41
alcohol, 42, 155
"Amazing Grace," 26-32, 90
ambassadors of hope, 163
anger, 41, 51, 54-57, 67-68, 86, 93, 94, 116, 120, 135, 138, 153, 154
animal kingdom, 98, 127
antidepressant medication, 155
applied psychology, 74, 79
armor, 78-79, 122-23
assertiveness training, 108
attachment, 100, 124, 154-55
attitudes, 29, 42, 44, 45, 53, 119, 120, 121, 151, 156
attribution errors, 119-20
autism, 75
automatic thoughts, 95, 129
autonomy, 59, 85
average, 104, 117-19, 126
basic sciences in psychology, 74, 79
behavior, 16, 20, 22, 24, 25, 30, 36, 38, 42, 43, 44, 74, 83, 87, 95, 96, 98, 101, 102, 106, 108, 109, 111, 112, 115, 129, 131, 133, 137, 150, 151, 152, 154, 156, 162
belief perseverance, 137, 139-40
biblical counseling, 12, 15-22, 32, 75, 109, 115, 123, 124, 141, 145, 157, 158, 159, 161
bitterness, 29, 68, 88, 153, 157
breathing training, 75, 107, 108
Bruce Almighty, 67
busyness, 87, 153
Calvinists, 67 138
care of souls, 17, 141
cheap grace, 62-64

childhood, 44, 49, 50, 51, 60, 81, 106, 112, 123, 130, 134, 138, 153, 154
Christian anthropology, 17
Christian Association for Psychological Studies, 16, 26
Christian community, 110, 112, 140, 144-45
Christian Counseling and Education Foundation, 16, 158
Christian mysticism, 88, 143
church, 12, 16, 17, 18, 26, 27, 28, 31, 37, 50, 53, 58, 62, 64, 89, 92, 99, 105, 116, 138, 139, 140-45, 146, 147, 149, 155
clinical psychology, 15, 16, 26, 33, 78
cogito, ergo sum, 135
cognitive challenges, 128
cognitive system, 76-77
cognitive therapy, 98, 106, 128, 129, 130, 133, 144
cognitive-behavioral psychology, 33, 75, 97
cognitive-experiential self theory, 76-77
collaborative empiricism, 144
common grace, 52, 53-57, 82, 107
community, 29, 30, 35, 90, 97, 110, 112, 122, 140-45, 146, 148, 162
community of grace, 140-45, 146
compassion, 15, 25, 33, 35, 36, 41, 45, 46, 53, 56, 62, 70, 81, 82, 116, 155, 156, 157, 162
condemnation, 22, 55, 65, 114, 119, 150
confession, 19, 46, 83, 112, 114, 115, 124, 157
confirmation bias, 17, 137, 138-39, 140
confrontation, 24, 36, 49, 51, 55, 56, 61, 65, 73, 77, 79, 85, 87, 92, 111, 112, 120, 122, 135, 138
contrition, 62, 80, 91, 149
conviction, 55, 80, 157, 160
core beliefs, 95, 129, 131, 152
costly grace, 62-63
Council of Carthage, 64
covenant, 23, 156
creation, 19, 23, 24, 30, 36, 39, 44, 46, 48, 50, 57, 60, 69, 70, 81, 82, 89, 90, 97, 98, 103, 104, 105, 108, 109, 125, 136, 149, 156
crime, 18, 23, 27, 44, 78, 105, 112-13
criticism, 17, 44, 55, 58, 74, 90, 94, 120, 138, 149, 153, 161

daily event planning, 108
decatastrophizing, 108
defenses, 49, 50, 51, 77-81, 90, 118, 122, 135, 137, 160
denial, 57, 63, 78
depression, 34, 39, 40, 54, 68, 69, 84, 86, 93, 110, 113, 115, 124, 129, 130, 133, 153, 155, 156
discovery, 50-53, 54, 55, 56, 64, 66, 67, 68, 72, 79, 143, 144, 152, 153, 160
distorted thinking, 133
divorce, 78, 84, 94, 95, 98, 99, 105, 125, 159
dopamine, 40
dysfunctional thought record, 108
eating disorders, 80, 133
ecclesiology, 17, 141
Eden, 19, 39, 40, 41, 50, 63, 72, 86, 88, 103, 104, 110
Educational Testing Service, 117
egoism, 133, 134, 135-40, 144, 145
electroconvulsive therapy, 155
emissaries of grace, 71
emotion-focused reflection, 135
empathy, 12, 33, 34-38, 40, 41, 42, 43, 45, 46, 47, 50, 54, 68, 70, 155, 156
existentialism, 54, 74, 79, 88, 155
experiential system, 76-77
experiments, 144
exploring the unexplored, 108
exposure techniques, 75, 108
faithfulness, 27, 30, 59, 67, 71, 82, 100, 121, 137, 140, 144, 162
fallen, 19, 22, 23, 37, 39, 40, 44, 59, 63, 79, 82, 84, 88, 89, 90, 92, 94, 96, 104, 108, 110, 134, 136, 150, 154
false self, 86
family systems, 33, 50
fear, 54, 57, 89, 94, 99, 107, 113, 129, 135, 148, 151
finitude, 136
forgiveness, 12, 19, 22, 45-47, 49, 56, 61, 62, 67-68, 71, 80, 82, 83, 92, 110, 114, 137, 140, 151, 157
free will, 67
functional domain, 97, 102, 103-25
fundamentalism, 22, 112, 141, 156
general revelation, 124

gentle correction, 120
global economy, 28
gospel, 24, 30, 63, 81, 100, 150, 156
grace, three dimensions of, 145-47, 154-61
gratitude, 53, 93
grief, 64, 68, 110, 112-13, 124, 149
guilt, 16, 28, 45, 46-47, 71, 80, 90, 93, 110, 112
healing relationships, 71, 161
heart, 26, 28, 29, 30, 31, 38, 39, 41, 49, 60, 67, 68, 76, 77, 82, 104, 109, 110, 111, 113, 114, 115, 116-22, 134, 136, 143, 146, 148, 151, 155
heaven, 37, 50, 53, 57, 63, 64, 89, 90, 123, 125, 127, 157
hiding, 54, 55, 57, 122, 150
holiness, 19, 24, 26, 31, 57, 59, 63, 64, 93, 100, 150, 151, 158
hope, 12, 18, 19, 20, 21, 31, 32, 41, 48, 51, 58, 59, 62, 64, 70, 77, 82, 83, 86, 88, 89, 93, 98, 105, 106, 113, 114, 115, 116, 122, 125, 136, 141, 144, 146, 151, 155, 159, 162, 163
hospital, 141, 155
human dignity, 35-36, 124
human nature, 22, 41, 77, 97, 133
human worth, 36
humility, 42, 63, 119, 121, 146, 150, 155, 157
humorous counters, 108
idolatry, 111, 113, 115, 116, 117, 123, 155
idols of the heart, 115, 155
illegal drugs, 105, 155
imago Dei, 23, 36, 50, 97, 98, 100
immediacy, 108
imposter, 61, 69
incarnation, 63, 84, 100
informed consent, 96
inherent sinfulness, 39-41
integrationists, 15, 16, 22, 109, 115, 140, 161
Integrative Psychotherapy, 12, 92-102, 106, 130, 132, 146, 151-54
intellectualization, 79
intelligence, 103, 117
intermediate beliefs, 129, 131, 152
interoceptive exposure, 75
interpersonal grace, 57, 146
interpersonal therapy, 100, 107
intimacy, 41, 63, 150, 153, 156, 162

isolation, 44, 54, 70, 87, 88 91, 124, 140
Journal of Biblical Counseling, 16, 17
Journal of Psychology and Christianity, 16
Journal of Psychology and Theology, 15
joy, 24, 62, 77, 88, 89, 90, 97, 105, 113, 116, 126, 139, 145, 157
justification, 24, 41, 53, 57, 64, 65, 67, 71, 113, 151, 157
kindness, mercy and grace, 58-59
Les Misérables, 65-66
listening for feelings, 108
Logos, 82
loneliness, 54, 77, 86-90, 91, 110, 159
looking inward, 144
maladaptive schemas, 130-31, 134, 152, 159
medication, 40, 93, 154, 155
menu-oriented approach to faith, 62
mercy ministries, 106
metaphysics, 74, 90, 96
moral counseling, 162
moral depravity, 59-62
mystery, 70, 81
natural and spiritual explanations, 122-25
natural error, 122
neurotransmitters, 59
Nicene Creed, 144
noble ruins, 37
non posse non peccare, 36
nouthetic counseling, 16, 162
object relations, 33, 95, 100, 162
old self/new self, 71, 130, 146
ontology, 23, 98, 100, 127, 128, 130, 145
oppression, 28, 41, 115
original sin, 23, 36, 37, 39, 40, 41, 46, 131
overconfidence, 137-38, 139, 140
paradox, 47, 48, 49, 69, 86, 108, 124
parenting, 42, 49, 56, 58, 59, 60, 83, 85, 94, 99, 105, 113, 117, 122, 124, 125, 132, 133, 134, 138, 139, 148, 149, 153
pastoral counseling, 16, 18, 106
pastors, 11, 16, 25, 84
pornography, 23, 87, 105, 110, 112, 124
posse non peccare, 37, 64
postmodernism, 138, 145
preaching, 22, 39, 30, 31, 49, 86, 114
predestination, 67
pride, 30, 51, 78, 103, 105, 113, 116-25, 136,

137, 140, 145, 155
probability estimates, 108
prodigal son, 100, 151, 157
projection, 78-79
psychiatry, 19, 155
Puritan prayer, 18-19
queries, 106, 160
racism, 28, 41, 44, 84, 94, 105
rationalization, 79
reconciliation, 57, 63-64, 83, 114, 163
recovery, 19, 21, 50-53, 54, 68, 72, 113, 125, 158
Recursive Schema Activation, 130-32
redemption, 12, 19, 22, 46, 48, 63, 64, 89, 92, 112, 113, 114, 137, 151, 155
reflection and restatement, 108
Reformers, 135
regression, 79
relational domain, 100, 102, 108, 111, 148-63
relationship factors, 154
relaxation training, 107, 108
repentance, 19, 26, 32, 46, 49, 55, 64, 83, 110, 111, 114, 124, 148, 149, 151, 156, 157, 158, 160, 161
repentance-friendly relationships, 157, 160
repression, 52, 79, 154
resentment, 68, 98, 113, 153, 157
retributive justice, 59, 62-64
righteousness, 44, 57, 63, 64, 82, 123, 125, 157
role-playing counters, 107, 108
sanctification, 12, 24, 41, 48, 53, 55, 57, 64, 67, 71, 72, 84, 93, 113, 151, 157, 158
scaling, 108
schemas, 98, 128-35, 146, 152, 159, 161
self-affirmation, 42
self-assessments, 117-19, 121
self-esteem, 18, 26, 42, 59, 60, 61, 62, 69, 83, 116, 133
self-examination, 26
self-interest, 28, 41, 42, 44, 55, 95, 125, 156
selfishness, 18, 44, 56, 145, 149, 151, 156
self-pity, 46
self-serving, 117, 144, 154
self-talk, 42, 62, 112, 113-14, 124, 129
seminary, 11, 15, 16, 35, 39, 49, 75, 149
serotonin, 18, 40, 88

sexism, 41
shalom, 63, 113
shame, 16, 25, 33, 36, 42, 45-47, 51, 57, 83, 87, 114, 125, 130, 135, 145, 148-50, 156
shoplifting, 148-49
sin
    Augustinian view of, 12, 23, 36-37, 39, 46, 91, 116, 118-19
    consequences of, 24, 25, 33, 38, 39, 42-45, 46, 62, 63, 67, 88, 110, 111, 124, 149, 150, 154, 159-61
    forensic view of, 12, 23
    macro and micro view of, 109-11
    noetic effects of, 51, 136, 137
    Pelagian view of, 36-37, 64
    personal, 33, 39, 93, 109-11, 114, 123, 133, 159
    relational view of, 12, 23, 44, 54, 149-50, 151, 152, 156, 159, 162
    three dimensions of, 38-45, 154-61
    toggle-switch view of, 38-39
    sexual, 19, 20, 28, 44, 87, 105, 113, 115, 155, 159
sinful choices, 41-42
skills-focused counseling, 162
slave trading, 27-31
social support, 124, 141
social work, 16
sovereignty of God, 59, 66-68

special grace, 12, 52, 53, 57-59
special revelation, 124
spiritual impotence, 59, 64-66
spirituality, 12, 60, 73, 74-77, 81, 86-90, 113, 154
splitting, 79
stress, 34, 79, 94, 95, 96, 102, 105, 110, 124, 153
structural domain, 98, 99, 126-47
systematic theology, 17, 40, 136
tabula rasa, 133
technology and loneliness, 86-87
therapeutic culture, 18, 27, 123, 162
three domain approach, 12, 97, 101, 102
total depravity, 47
toxic faith, 141
transcendence, 81-82
true self, 61, 86
victim, 153
virtue, 42, 60, 62, 68, 82, 84, 86, 87, 119, 162
volition, 42, 69, 93
Wesleyans, 98, 150
Westminster Seminary, 15
Wheaton College, 15, 58, 92
white noise, 38-41
wisdom, 25, 35, 57, 89, 120, 144, 145
Wonderful Counselor, 155
worldview, 19, 74, 75, 96, 109, 130, 133

Scripture Index

Genesis
1:27, *36*
1:27-29, *97, 100*
3:1-7, *149*

2 Chronicles
7:14-15, *157*

Psalms
51:5, *23*

Proverbs
14:29, *55*
15:1, *55*
15:1-2, *120*
15:18, *55*

Isaiah
9:6, *155*
53:6, *156*
65:5, *119*

Matthew
5:21-22, *55*
5:28, *115*
5:8, *115*
6:14-15, *46*
6:21, *115*
13:15, *115*
15:19-20, *115*
18:21-35, *46*

22:37, *115*
22:37-40, *116*

Mark
11:23, *115*

Luke
2:52, *53*
4:22, *53*
14:7, *119*
15:11-32, *151*
15:17, *157*
18:13, *90*
24:32, *115*

John
1:1-4, *121*
1:14, *32, 63, 81, 82,
    84, 100, 121,
    140, 154*
8:11, *65*

Romans
2:19-20, *119*
3:23-24, *57*
5:6-11, *150*
5:7-8, *59*
5:20-21, *24*
6:6, *130*
6:17, *53*
7:14-25, *109*

8:20-23, *63, 79*
8:28, *79*
12:3, *53, 118*
15:7, *65, 146*

1 Corinthians
16:3, *53*

Galatians
2:20-21, *71*
2:21, *57*
5:19-20, *55*

Ephesians
2:4-5, *136*
2:4-7, *57*
2:8, *136*
3:16-21, *147*
4:22-24, *130*
4:26, *55*
4:27, *55*
4:31, *55*
6:11-14, *123*

Philippians
1:6, *30*
2:3, *119*
2:5-8, *121*

Colossians
1:15, *62, 82*

1:17, *70*
1:19-22, *64*
1:22, *24*
1:27, *163*
3:9-11, *130*
3:13, *157*

2 Timothy
1:9, *57*

Titus
3:5, *64*

Hebrews
1:3, *62*
11:13, *88, 89*
11:14-16, *89*
12:1-3, *145*

James
1:19-20, *55*

1 Peter
1:13, *53*

1 John
1:8-9, *137*
4:18, *151*

CAPS

An Association for Christian Psychologists,
Therapists, Counselors and Academicians

CAPS is a vibrant Christian organization with a rich tradition. Founded in 1956 by a small group of Christian mental health professionals, chaplains and pastors, CAPS has grown to more than 2,100 members in the U.S., Canada and more than 25 other countries.

CAPS encourages in-depth consideration of therapeutic, research, theoretical and theological issues. The association is a forum for creative new ideas. In fact, their publications and conferences are the birthplace for many of the formative concepts in our field today.

CAPS members represent a variety of denominations, professional groups and theoretical orientations; yet all are united in their commitment to Christ and to professional excellence.

CAPS is a non-profit, member-supported organization. It is led by a fully functioning board of directors, and the membership has a voice in the direction of CAPS.

CAPS is more than a professional association. It is a fellowship, and in addition to national and international activities, the organization strongly encourages regional, local and area activities which provide networking and fellowship opportunities as well as professional enrichment.

To learn more about CAPS, visit www.caps.net.

CAPS Books
from IVP Academic

The joint publishing venture between IVP Academic and CAPS aims to promote the understanding of the relationship between Christianity and the behavioral sciences at both the clinical/counseling and the theoretical/research levels. These books will be of particular value for students and practitioners, teachers and researchers.

For more information, visit InterVarsity Press's website at www.ivpress.com and type *Christian Association for Psychological Studies* into the search box in the upper right corner of the screen.